Gary Elson and Oliver Lucanus

The Barbs Aquarium

Everything About Natural History,
Purchase, Health, Care, Breeding,
and Species Identification

Filled with Full-color Photographs
Illustrations by Michele Earle-Bridges

BARRON'S

CONTENTS

An Intriguing Family · 5

What Are Barbs? 5

Classification of Barbs 6

Barbs Are Carp 7

Classification System 10

The Barb Aquarium · 13

Barb Behavior 13

Size of the Tank 13

Shape and Height of
the Tank 14

The Stand 14

Heating 15

Lighting 16

Stocking Barb Tanks 17

The Traditional Community
Tank Versus the Biotope
Aquarium 18

HOW-TO: Running a
Healthy Aquarium 22

Water · 25

Water Chemistry 25

Water Hardness 26

Filtration 26

Aquascaping · 33

Setting Up the Tank 33

Setups for Different Fish 34

Plants · 37

Types of Plants 37

Feeding Your Barbs · 45

Overfeeding 45

Types of Food 45

How Much and How
Often to Feed 47

Vacations 47

Health and Fitness · 49

The Retailer 49

When You Are Ready
to Buy 51

Making Sure Your Fish
Stay Healthy 51

Common Diseases 54

Precautions 56

HOW-TO: Breeding Barbs 58

Barb Groups	61
Asian *Barbus* Species	61
African *Barbus*	70
Danios	72
Rasboras	78
Loaches	85
Stonesuckers	87
Algae Eaters	87
The Giant Barbs and "Sharks"	90
Conclusion	92
Information	**93**
Index	94

AN INTRIGUING FAMILY

5

Barbs, like the waters they come from, are things of movement. In the home aquarium, these active, inquisitive creatures are always exploring, chasing, and, for their keeper, performing. But while we can say barbs are energetic, that very energy makes it hard for us to say what a "barb" is.

What Are Barbs?

This manual will look at a fraction of the species of barbs and their relatives that exist in the wild. For fishkeepers, other popular groups such as cichlids, gouramies, and tetras, are often limited mainly by availability. Barbs are limited by the number of species appropriate for the home aquarium. While the group has many rare and much-sought-after members, most species that aren't kept are unpopular because they aren't easy to keep. There is very little long-term home aquarium interest in *Myxocyprinus asiaticus,* for example, an attractive (when young) Chinese species that can reach 2 feet (61 cm) in length, or in the unattractive but impressive *Catlocarpio siamensis,* which can hit a healthy 10 feet (305 cm). For almost the opposite reasons,

Rasboras are caught in slow moving waters such as these.

tiny barbs such as Africa's delicate *Barbus jae* (1.5 inches [4 cm]) are only sporadically available. They have remained specialist fish for those who like micro fish tanks, and have never developed the following their delicate beauty should call for. Some of the *Phoxinus* species (the red-bellied dace) of North America are spectacular in their beauty when captured in the wild, but that coldwater beauty fades in the uncomfortable warmth of the indoor home aquarium. Once we factor in the enormous number of barb species that have found survival in sunlight-reflecting silver coloration, we can see that a large percentage of barbs fall outside the scope of an aquarium manual. Barbs can offer too many contrasts for the average fishkeeper!

As a result of our having to divide barbs not on sound scientific principles, but rather on aquarium interest, a manual like this cannot be considered a scientific work. We know about

Families

The order Cypriniformes (carplike fish) has five families:

✔ The Balitoridae (Balatorinae and Nemacheilinae) includes the stonesuckers discussed in this book.

✔ The Catostomidae, the suckers native to North America.

✔ The popular Cobitidae, or loaches.

✔ The Cyprinidae, including the barbs and rasboras and the main focus of the book.

✔ The Gyrinocheilidae, including the Chinese algae eater discussed in this book.

the family, and recognize that they are a vibrant, often rambunctious bunch, but our job as aquarium hobbyists is to pick and choose which members we spend our time with. As if to compensate, the species we will look at in this manual are among the most active, colorful, and hardy animals in the hobby.

Classification of Barbs

Barbs belong to the larger grouping of Cypriniformes, and Cypriniformes are a large part of the world's fish fauna, not only in tropical environments, but also in a band across the northern half of the planet. They do not inhabit high Arctic regions, nor are they naturally found in South America, the Australasian region, or Madagascar. However, human intervention has had its effect, as a fish such as China's *Tanichthys albonubes* (the white cloud minnow) now has introduced breeding populations in Colombia and Madagascar. This large family has spread through the waters of Asia, Africa, North America, and Europe with the energy of a school of danios spreading through a home aquarium. In so doing, they have undergone an evolutionary explosion, turning into fish of all sizes and shapes, in many different river systems. Among the many varied body plans they offer us are those of *Barbus,* danios, loaches, minnows, rasboras, and carp. What does a secretive, snakelike kuhli loach have in common with a lumbering goldfish, a darting danio, or an ever-enthusiastic rosy barb? We could say "family," although the relationships can be distant. Or we could approach them as this book will by saying they are popular tropical-aquarium fish linked closely enough by a common ancestry to be considered together in an aquarium manual. We will look at this marvelously complex group based on the following simple criteria:

✔ Are they a reasonable size for the average home aquarium?

There is no mistaking the alert look of a healthy barb.

Barb species are found in many parts of the world, including Asia.

✔ Can they prosper in indoor temperatures?
✔ Are they popular, have they been popu-lar in the past, or could they become popular?

Barbs Are Carp

"Carp" is a loaded word, but, as much as aquarists hate to admit it, it is what barbs are. Carp are popular food fish in many cultures, and despised artificially introduced destroyers of ecosystems in others. These bulky eating machines aren't what we would think of as aquarium fish, with good reason, but the body model of the carp is the essential barb form, especially for the popular aquarium species. The top and bottom of the body tends to follow the same plan, curved, moderately high-bodied, and balanced.

Teeth: The toothless mouth is mobile, and can protrude to draw food in toward the teeth, which are situated in the throat. The teeth themselves are extremely important, even though aquarists never see them. While the external characteristics of two species may appear almost identical, the pharyngeal (throat) teeth will have different forms, depending on the diet of the fish. Mollusk eaters, algae eaters, and generalists all have differently formed teeth. As far as external body plans go, in many cases, one size fits all. It is the pharyngeal teeth that often differentiate species.

Scales and head: The scales on the fish are large, but the head is bare.

Barbels: Most Cyprinids (but not all) have a pair of barbels, hence the popular aquarium name.

Fins: The caudal (tail) fin is forked, and there is no adipose fin, a fin found on many characins, between the dorsal and the caudal.

The Tiger Barbs

The tiger barb is a longtime favorite, but what is it? Three distinct but similar species have been known to show up under this name; the most common is *Barbus tetra-zona*, from Indonesia, Sumatra, and Borneo. This barb is a staple at fish farms. However, wild imports of *Barbus pentazona penta-zona*, the more slender-bodied softwater five-banded barb from Southeast Asia, Sin-gapore, the Malayan Peninsula, and Borneo, could also be traveling under this name. *Barbus partipentazona* from Thailand has also been imported as a "tiger barb." All of these barbs have different needs. Latin names are useful!

The wild or common phase of the Half Stripe Barb (Barbus semifasciolatus).

The Longnose Barb (Barbus dorsalis).

The Cherry Barb (Barbus titteya) *is popular in the aquarium hobby, but endangered in the wild.*

African Spotted Barbs are difficult to identify, as there are many species.

The Eight-Banded Barb (Eirmotus octozona) *can be difficult to maintain in an aquarium.*

The Three-Spotted Barb (Barbus eburneensis).

Barbus macrops, *a rare African barb.*

The Leopard or Frankei Danio is probably an aquarium-developed, mutant form.

Barbus caudovittatus *is a rare visitor from Cameroon.*

The popular Pearl Danio (Danio albolineatus).

Barbus trimaculatus *from Guinea.*

Danio choprai *is a recently imported danio from Northern Thailand. It should become a staple in the aquarium hobby.*

Classification System

Nature has not been rigid with barbs, and every human rule about animals has exceptions when held up to reality. What we can work with is the time-honored system of classification originally worked out by the Swedish botanist Carl Linnaeus in the late eighteenth century. To simplify greatly, in this classification system, all living creatures are assigned to a genus, and are then given a species name; for example, humans are *Homo sapiens*. The genus is capitalized, while the species name always appears with the first letter in the lower case. Subspecies names can follow *(Homo sapiens*

━━━ CHECKLIST ━━━

Goldfish

Goldfish may be the most popular member of this family, but they probably shouldn't be.

1 *Carassius auratus* (Linnaeus 1758), in all its familiar artificially selected goldfish forms, is a coolwater bruiser that can grow to well over a foot (30 cm).

2 Its vegetable-based diet and messy digestive system make it a terrible candidate for small tanks, unless the keeper changes water constantly.

3 Goldfish can live for years under atrocious conditions, but the great question is whether they should have to. They are much better suited to life as pond fish.

sapiens), as can information on local origins, populations, and so on. At the end of the name, we find the name of the individual who described the creature, and the year of the description, added to help us locate the original description should we wish to read it. This flexible system uses Latin. While that dead language was better known to Linnaeus and his European colleagues in the eighteenth century than it is to modern readers, it still serves us well as a neutral language belonging to no one. English-speaking hobbyists may often express frustration at Latin names, but the language is equally obscure to all who haven't studied it, no matter what their language or origin. Given that every language has its own popular names for fish, and that even within languages, names can vary by region, or be used for many species—how many different "glass barbs" are there?—a little effort to learn Latin names can save you a lot of trouble in the long run, as well as increasing your chances of finding information on a fish that interests you.

Name Changes

An area where scientific and hobbyist needs clash is the changing nature of names. If one looks at older books, the tendency was to "park" species under a convenient name that at least gave a general picture of what the newly discovered animal was. As research has finally been done on individual species, new genus names are proposed based on new knowledge and often accepted (or not) within the scientific community. These name changes can be a source of confusion. The names of aquarium barbs have not been as affected as the names for other popular, and therefore more seriously studied, aquarium groups, but recent research clarifying the relationships between different barbs has already begun to change some time-honored names. The authors have decided to sidestep this question by leaving the majority of aquarium barbs under the old umbrella genus of *Barbus,* thereby avoiding the confusing scientific controversies about validity of the genera *Puntius, Systomus,* and *Capoeta.* However, there are a number of names in the *Rasbora* group that will be new for many aquarists.

Undescribed Species

The question of undescribed species is another sticking point. Apparently "new" fish are often found by hobbyists/explorers/collectors who do not wish to take on the research and training necessary to produce an accepted and valid scientific description. If a fish is found that the discoverer figures is most likely a new rasbora, for example, it will receive a temporary name, as *Rasbora* species, usually shortened to "*Rasbora sp.*" A temporary tag will follow, giving us names such as *Rasbora sp.* "whatever." At best, the temporary name will be based on a place name for the collection locality or a defining physical characteristic, but if the discoverer is in the fish business, the name will often be a not very helpful marketing device. Keepers of cichlids have a lot of experience of new but ugly species being tagged with wildly inappropriate but very

A Weird and Wonderful Barb

One of the weirdest relationships between humans and Cypriniformes is the wondrous case of *Garra rufa* (Heckel 1843). This 5-inch (13-cm) carplike fish from the River Jordan, the Tigris-Euphrates River basin, Syria, and Turkey is kept in aquariums, but usually not by hobbyists. One population from a Turkish hot spring has reportedly been nibbling at bathers since time immemorial. These fish are now being marketed as an alternative therapy for a variety of skin ailments, based on their ability to gently nibble away diseased or flaking skin. This traditional medicine has attracted commercial attention. The backers of the new *Garra rufa* industry say the fish allow for new healthy skin growth because of chemicals they secrete while eating. How scientifically based this is may be an open question, but live *Garra rufa* are now being marketed in Europe as an alternative therapy for skin disease.

appealing names, and the same can happen with barbs. When you acquire such a fish, expect its name to change as soon as it is studied. Also be aware that our little aquarium fish are not of great economic importance, and their study is not always a priority to those who fund research. Temporary names can be around for a long time.

THE BARB AQUARIUM

Barbs offer us some very beautiful choices for the home aquarium. The problem for many aquarists, especially for those new to this hobby, is how we define "choices." Too often, we take the narrow focus, and look at how many fish we can cram into our tanks. One lone barb in a desktop microtank is no more interesting than 30 in a tank built for 10. In both cases, the fish can't behave as active, living animals, and will not remain alive simply as ornaments.

Barb Behavior

We want to be able to enjoy and admire the diversity of fish shapes and colors, but in doing this, we often forget to consider barb behavior. What our barbs do, and how much we enjoy keeping them, depends on what conditions we offer them—and how we set up our fish tanks depends on what we want from our window into aquatic life.

As we have noted, barbs and movement go together. Most of the popular species swim fast, and they swim often. Most are stream fish, used to the possibilities the complex network of small, often heavily vegetated water systems around the flow of great rivers have to offer. However, there are others that prefer more

*Signal Rasboras (**Rasbora dorsioccelata**) are emerald eyed beauties that look especially well in dimly lit tanks.*

placid environments, and can be found in seasonally isolated ponds, ditches, and swamps. Small barbs need hiding places for a sense of security, while their larger cousins want water they can restlessly roam around in. There are a few different aquarium setups that can be used.

Size of the Tank

The first general rule for successfully keeping most fish is to purchase the largest aquarium that space and finances will allow. The larger the aquarium, the more stable it is as an environment. While a big tank may look like work, the small aquariums are the ones that demand the most attention. The maintenance of an aquarium is not time consuming, but it should be done regularly. The popular barbs are usually heavy and messy eaters. In a small tank, fish waste and uneaten food accumulate quickly, polluting the water. If a hobbyist is not prepared to follow a consistent maintenance schedule, the fish will suffer. A larger tank still needs to be cleaned, but its greater water volume will be more forgiving. While giving your barbs room to run, it will also allow for more plants, and, what is important for most hobbyists, more fish.

Shape and Height of the Tank

With the possible exception of hexagonal tanks, with their lack of swimming room, the shape of the tank is not important. Your best bet is to opt for an aquarium with a large base. Depth is not that important, unless you want one of the giant tinfoil barb-type fish, as long as a lower height does not detract from the visibility of the tank's inhabitants. Many barbs come from shallow water habitats in the wild, but all are happy at all the depths available for home aquariums. You want to be able to observe your school, or schools, of barbs in movement. Providing swimming room should be your primary goal.

The Stand

You will need to find a strong, sturdy, and attractive stand. Remember that a gallon (3.8 L) of water weighs approximately 8 pounds (3.8 kg), and plan accordingly. If you choose to place your aquarium on a table or a bookshelf, take into consideration the unavoidable small spills that go with water changes and aquarium maintenance. Barb behavior can be a problem too. One of the authors once kept a school of *Barbus conchonius* (rosy barbs) that greeted the (artificial) light of every morning by energetically splashing water in a 2-foot (61–cm) radius around their tank, which was rapidly supplied with a very tight cover.

Weight and Surface of the Stand

Only very large aquariums can be a challenge to the strength of your floors, but smaller aquariums can be too much for some tables or bookcases, especially over time. Make sure that the stand you use doesn't wobble. A water-filled tank should not move, as this will put undue pressure on its silicone sealant. An aquarium in movement, or a tank that is lifted without being fully drained, will often spring leaks. Conveniently, you can find a wide variety of well-designed and attractive aquarium stands in any good aquarium store. Make certain your tank is placed on a level surface. Many fishkeepers will add insurance by putting styrofoam sheets or strips of foam-backed carpeting under their tanks to help absorb any unevenness under their aquariums.

The barb aquarium.

Location

Fish-watching, most likely the true goal of this exercise, is best done from the comfort of an armchair. This brings us to the all-important question of aquarium location.

Quiet: Your tank should be in a quiet place where you can be comfortable observing it. It should be a low-traffic area, so that the fish are not constantly frightened by passing people. Fish are very sensitive to vibrations passing through their water, so jumping children or booming stereos can be quite stressful to them. Barbs can become quite jumpy, literally.

Light: It is important to place your aquarium close to the necessary electrical outlet. It is also a good idea to carefully consider where your tank will be in relation to your doors and windows. Barbs look astonishing in natural sunlight; however, when you can't see your fish because of algae growing on the glass, the benefits of natural light will be less appealing. Constantly scraping algae off the glass is a chore to be avoided (see page 22), as are the scratches on the glass that go with it. Diffused sunlight in a bright room is not going to give your tank problems, and it will accentuate the colors of many barbs. However, many aquarists like to keep their tank in areas where only the lights in the hood illuminate the aquarium. A common compromise is to set a light timer so the tank gets a short period of diffused natural sunlight in the morning, and artificial light for the rest of the day.

Heating and air conditioning: It is also best not to place an aquarium too close to a heating vent or system, or an air conditioner. Concentrated but uneven blasts of heat or cold can affect the accuracy of your aquarium's heater, which can cause water temperature fluctuations and, on occasion, jammed heater thermostats. You, as the fishkeeper, should try to maintain consistency in the environment you offer to your fish.

Household products: Household products can be problematic for all fish tanks. Note that a kitchen is a bad location, due to cooking residues settling on the surface of the water.

✔ You should be careful about using household sprays, soaps, cleaners, or chemicals where they can get into the water.

✔ Insecticides are obviously deadly.

✔ One often overlooked problem can be the use of ammonia-based glass cleaners on aquariums. Toxic ammonia, as you will see in the section on filtration (page 26), is a major problem in fish tanks.

Heating

Not all barbs need warm water, but for most, a good heater becomes necessary. Don't make the error of buying a cut-rate heater, as this is an area of aquarium technology where quality is of the utmost importance. A first-rate electronic submersible heater will cost more than a hang-on-the-back clip-on heater; however, it will be much more efficient. No technical factor will change the environment your cold-blooded fish live in more quickly and radically than a heater breakdown. The best-case scenario for a heater malfunction has it shut off, dropping the temperature rapidly and probably creating the perfect conditions for an outbreak of "ich" (see diseases section, page 54). The worst cases involve uncontrolled heating of the water, creating fish soup, or causing the glass tube on the heater to crack, exposing the hobbyist to the risk of a serious electrical shock.

Electronic submersible heaters can be very reliable, something you may not find with the cheaper models on the market. They also allow for a tighter aquarium cover, a key consideration with active leapers like barbs.

Under average circumstances, the general recommendation is for 3 to 5 watts of heater strength per gallon (3.8 L) of water. Many aquarists will put two heaters in a tank, as insurance in case one breaks down.

A trustworthy thermometer is another necessity, to allow you to monitor the efficiency of your heater.

Lighting

Lighting is almost a book in itself. Keeping planted aquariums is an engrossing hobby that can easily be combined with barb keeping. Many of our fish revel in bright light, while plants can help filter aquarium water.

Generally, fluorescent lighting is recommended for small- to medium-sized aquariums,

Chela laubaca, one of the many flying barbs.

CHECKLIST

Electrical Safety

1 Make certain all electrical appliances used for aquariums are secured from falling into the water.

2 Those that do come into contact with the water should be approved by the standards association of your country.

3 All electrical appliances should be disconnected before the aquarist puts his or her hands into the water.

The tiny, luminous White Cloud Minnow (Tanichthys albonubes).

with different intensities, depending on tank size and plant choice. Older aquarium hoods with incandescent fixtures still do a reasonable job, although it is necessary to experiment to see which plants will prosper under their reduced light spectrum. Incandescents cost more to run, and generate a lot of heat, but they still have a following. Many fans of slow-growing, tough-leaved, low-light cryptocorynes and *Anubias* favor combinations of incandescent and fluorescent bulbs. Aquarists can also go in the opposite direction, and investigate the wonderful possibilities of high-tech, high-intensity lighting systems, popularized by the saltwater reef hobby, but these systems usually become attractive to those who become serious plant keepers.

Whatever system you choose, do not skimp on lighting for a barb tank, as these fish are spectacular under the right illumination. A quick look at the often brilliant silver on their scales shows most of them to be fish that seek refuge and camouflage in brightly lit, open water.

Note: For fluorescent systems, another great investment is a simple light timer. By being able to regulate the time of your lighting even when you aren't present, you will be able to both provide a more stable environment for fish and grow plants.

Stocking Barb Tanks

Sometimes, it can be good to look at schooling fish such as barbs as communities first and individuals second. Barbs live in groups, and in the wild (and the evolutionary history of the animal), the group is essential to the survival of the individual. This may have developed as a protection against predators that will never be present in your home, but it has serious consequences for the social needs of these gregarious creatures. Most barbs live in roaming hierarchical groups, and spend a lot of their time sorting out rank. Their tendency to nip at and spar with each other rarely does damage, and is part of their active natures.

Kept in groups of less than six, many popular barbs will often transfer their attention and behavioral patterns ("aggression") to non-barbs. This can stress their tankmates considerably, if it doesn't cause their deaths. Tiger barbs have an especially bad reputation in this regard. The "lone barb syndrome" has frustrated many a newcomer to these fish, given its ability to pop up in even peaceful species such as zebra danios.

Crowding

In trying to treat your barbs properly by buying schools of species, the desire to keep several species can lead you to jam your fish tank to the rafters. The problem is not just how visually unappealing an overly busy tank can be. Many people enjoy the bus station hustle and bustle of a crowded barb tank; however, overcrowding has serious consequences in a closed aquatic system. Levels of fish waste versus water volume easily get out of control. This, in turn, can take a lot of the fun out of fishkeeping, as your choice becomes constant water changes or dead fish. It is much better to set yourself the goal of keeping one small fish per gallon of water. This rule is imprecise, as a heavy-bodied tiger barb is a lot more fish than an inch (2.5 cm) of streamlined pearl danio or cherry barb. The rule favored by the authors is to calculate exactly how many fish you think your tank can safely hold, then put half as many in it. As with most advice, this is easier said than done.

The Traditional Community Tank Versus the Biotope Aquarium

The next major choice an aquarist has is the nature of the living community within the glass box. The great adaptability of the barb family makes it ideal for almost any sort of aquarium, but it also leaves the fishkeeper with lots of choices. Most of us opt for the traditional community tank, in which a variety of species from different places are kept together in one tank. The design of this living system should be based around the following principles.

Levels

Even in a relatively shallow aquarium, fish occupy different levels. The easiest way to view this is by thinking about flake food falling through the water, and where your fish like to strike at it. Most popular killifish and gouramies are found at the surface, while barbs, tetras, and other schooling fish like to swim in the mid ranges; loaches, catfish, and territorial cichlids are oriented to the bottom. Generally, a community tank keeper tries for a combination of species based not only on coloration, but also on niches within the aquarium. Remember that barbs are anything but rigid in their needs. More than many other groups, they will go where the food is, and compete with almost everything in the aquarium.

Shape

Fish are often kept for the visual display they offer as they interact. Even the smallest aquarium store will offer schools of torpedo-shaped, restless *Danio rerio* (zebra fish) to complement deeper-bodied *Barbus tetrazona* (tiger barbs) or

Barbus conchonius (rosy barb) types. Usually, schools of small fish are visually "framed" by the addition of larger heavy-bodied fish. Large-bodied, peaceful fish such as Asian gouramis are kept as a visual contrast/counterpoint to their smaller-bodied tankmates. The idea is to draw the viewer's attention to the contrast in fish shapes the aquarist has chosen. The art of creating living visual displays in an aquarium can be quite fascinating, which brings us to the next aspect of community tank planning.

Behavior

Many species of barb will shred inappropriately chosen tankmates such as angelfish *(Pterophyllum scalare)* or fancy Bettas *(Betta splendens)*. They can't resist the fins of these popular fish, and angels and Bettas can't resist the lightning attacks of more maneuverable barbs. Your barbs are not "mean," any more than an angel is when it decides to snack on a juvenile barb or tetra. In both cases, the fish-keeper has made an error in choosing incompatible fish.

Planning a tank means reading up on the species that interest you. Some barbs (especially of the genus *Barbus*) do like to nip, and should only be kept with robust, mobile, and short-finned tankmates. And, given barbs' energy levels, fish that prefer slow-moving, placid environments may find barbs annoying and stressful company.

Barbs can make excellent companions to many more robust species. The larger, stronger barbs (and Epalzeorhynchos) are popular as "dither" fish in cichlid tanks. A dither fish is used to draw out shy but potentially rough

Popular Aquarium Fish That Are Not Compatible with Barbus Species

Fish That Get Nipped
Betta splendens (Siamese Fighting Fish)
Pterophyllum scalare (Angelfish)
Poecilia reticulata (Fancy guppies)
Artificially selected long-finned forms of any aquarium fish

Fish That Will Be Stressed by Active Barb Species
Tanganyikan Cichlids
Pearl Gouramies
Dwarf Gouramies
Dwarf Cichlids

Fish That Kill Barbs
Malawi Cichlids
Any fish predator kept in the hobby; never buy a fish without reading about it first.

tankmates that can channel their territoriality and aggression toward robust, fast-swimming tankmates, without ever being able to actually harm them. T-barbs are often kept with larger cichlids, while rosy barbs play the same role with medium-sized Central American cichlids. Robust barbs can also get along famously with Australasian rainbowfish, South American tetras of equal size, Corydoras catfish, and most active live-bearer species. Another option is to keep mixed species tanks of different barbs. They can be a lot of fun to watch on their own.

These are males of a new arrival, the Orange Fin Danio (Danio kyathit).

The endangered Tiger Danio (Danio pathirana) *is only available to aquarists because of captive breeding programs.*

A female of the exciting new Orange Fin Danio.

Danio aequipinnatus, *one of the Giant Danios.*

The Spotted Danio (Danio nigrofasciatus) *is quieter than the Zebra, making it a good community fish.*

Hatchet Barbs (Chela dadyburjori) *are a good choice for a quiet community.*

The Asian Rummy-Nose (Sabwa resplendens) *loses its color in soft water.*

Microrasbora rubescens, *the Pink Dwarf Rasbora.*

A specimen of the recently discovered bright green "Somchai" Microrasbora.

Microrasbora erythromicron, *the Striped Dwarf Rasbora is a rare but attractive hardwater fish.*

Brigitte's Rasbora (Boraras brigittae) *is one of the smallest of the barb-type species.*

The Cardinal Rasbora (Sundadanio axelrodi) *is as beautiful as the popular Cardinal Tetra.*

Keeping an aquarium clean means keeping a flexible schedule and creating a relaxed routine. Certain tasks must be done, and as long as they are done regularly, they are easy. If ignored and left to become crises, they become the kind of work that discourages new hobbyists.

A water change is required once every week or two. Even the best filter only buys time. A routine change can be of anywhere from 20 (for an uncrowded aquarium) to 50 percent (for a crowded community tank) of the tank volume. The temperature of the new water must match the water temperature in the tank, and the new water must be treated with products (available in all good pet stores) to neutralize chlorine or chloramine.

Water changing is a chore; however, it is a quick one. Begin by unplugging heaters (which can break if their glass tubes heat up while unsubmerged). You can purchase a water changing system that uses a hose connected to your tap, and a swimming pool-type valve to add and remove water. A 2- or 5-gallon (7½–20 L) bucket and a siphon hose can also be used for changes. This bucket should be used only for your aquarium to avoid household chemical contamination, and chosen so it isn't too heavy to carry when filled.

It is wise to use a gravel cleaner (a tube attached to a siphon hose, available at any good aquarium store) when removing water. These inexpensive devices avoid the annoying problem of siphoning up gravel, while removing wastes that settle between the grains.

During changes, remove excess algae with a scraper. While present in all healthy tanks, as it is in nature, algae out of control is both a sign of trouble and a problem itself.

Green, threadlike algae is the bane of plant-keepers, as few algae eating fish will touch it. It is very hard to remove manually, and in the worst case scenario, will simply reappear as quickly as it is removed. Luckily, there is a species from the barb group that can come to the rescue (*Crossocheilus siamensis*).

Green algae explosions (especially green water) can come from overfeeding, poor maintenance, direct sunlight, and other maintenance related set-up problems.

Acclimatizing new fish.

HEALTHY AQUARIUM

If colonies of brown algae develop in a tank, it is a sign of too low light levels combined with nutrients (pollution) in the water. Black, hairlike algae is a troublesome pest on plants. Infested leaves must be removed. Strong smelling, slimy bluish-green algae is actually a bacteria known as Cyanobacter. It comes with water pollution, but is hard to eradicate. In poorly maintained tanks, it can be a real pest; however, once established, even water changes won't eliminate it. An old trick not often used today is turning off the aquarium lights, and darkening the tank for up to a week. Higher plants will survive, but quick growing algae can often be knocked into apparent dormancy.

Algicides are not recommended in closed aquarium systems. Chemical short cuts can build up quickly in the relatively small volume of a fishtank.

Add water either directly from an aquarium-safe hose (after adding any water treatment chemicals—in this case a necessity, not a short cut) or in the same bucket you just emptied. Use a plate, or a similar detergent-free plastic or glass object, on which to pour fresh water to avoid disturbing the gravel.

Even if your tank doesn't have algae, the inside glass will harbor considerable microscopic life. Wiping the glass with every water change will brighten your view of the aquarium considerably.

Each water change adds nutrients for your plants, but the addition of a good fertilizer specifically designed for aquarium use is

This is the proper method for siphoning tank water.

recommended at this point. It makes a difference, as does realizing fluorescent bulbs only nourish plants for about six months, so should be changed regularly. To keep track, either keep a log, or write the date of installation directly onto the ends of your fluorescent bulbs with a marker.

At each water change, do any necessary cleaning or changing of media inside filters. If you have many plants, take a moment to see that the intake tubes are clear.

WATER

Water is an amazing substance, which, as much as air, has more to it than meets the eye. Taking the time to learn about what comes from your tap may be important for your own health, but it is essential for the success of your aquarium.

Water Chemistry

There are a lot of barbs in nature, but a relatively limited number in the aquarium trade. In effect, the market has focused on those species that can prosper in the water available from most municipal and even well-water systems. The exceptions, the rain forest barb and *Rasbora* species from mineral-poor blackwater, are rarely encountered. Should you have the good fortune to find some in a shop, then research on the individual needs of the species will be required. In general though, the barbs we see are undemanding about water chemistry, unless we wish to breed them.

For those inclined to the study of chemistry, understanding the makeup of water may become a hobby in itself. For the average fish-keeper, it is important to learn about the composition of our local water supply, and choose fish that can live with the parameters we can reasonably offer. In many cases, a detailed

This fast flowing stream is a habitat of the popular T-barb.

breakdown can be supplied by your municipality, or as part of the testing of the water quality of a well. Beware though—the chemistry of water can change with the seasons, depending on rainfall, snow melt, or drought.

pH

The pH of water is another key concept. Put simply, it is the measure of the acidity or alkalinity of water. A pH of 7.0 is neutral—lower is more acidic, higher more alkaline. The differences between a pH of 7.0 and 6.0 are immense. Aquarium fish can come from water at a range between pH 4.0 and 9.5, with the great majority coming from between pH 6.0 and 8.0. In aquariums, most readily available barbs are happy in the 6.5 to 7.8 range.

Buffering

Buffering is the next key concept, especially for aquarists who wish to keep delicate rain forest barbs and *Rasbora*. Many of these fish need very acidic water, a rarity in the taps of most cities. Buffering is the ability of the mineral content of water to neutralize acids. Beware of the apparent convenience of the many chemical products sold to acidify your tank's water. If acidifying aquarium products are added to well-buffered water, the drop in pH will quickly be neutralized, and the pH will rapidly bounce back to its original level, or close. Such bounces in pH are extremely dangerous to your fish, and any use of these acids must be preceded by tests on water that contains no fish.

On the other hand, if you have a water supply that is extremely soft, you must be aware of buffering as well. Unbuffered water is prone to the dreaded "pH crash," a sudden drop in pH caused by the accumulation of acids produced by fish, plants, and closed aquatic systems in general. A pH crash can be fatal to your fish.

The bottom line is that water is not as simple a thing as we often assume it to be. A few minutes of research into your local conditions can mean the difference between your being a successful aquarist, and your constantly running back to the pet store to replace prized fish that seem to die for no identifiable reason

Minerals and Impurities

All local sources will have differing degrees of minerals and impurities in them. Some of these are beneficial or essential to our fish and plants. Generally, we talk about the hardness and softness of our water without realizing just how general and imprecise those terms are.

Water Hardness

Aquarium literature is full of references to water hardness, but the measures used vary, depending on the national origin of the author. There is no international hobbyist standard we can all safely refer to. In effect, water hardness is the measure of dissolved minerals in a water supply. The common methods for measurement do not discriminate between which minerals are present, but produce a broad and workable snapshot. Most hobbyist test kits will simply measure parts per million (ppm). Mineral-poor water is usually associated with areas of high rainfall (very important for rain forest species), while harder water develops through consistent longer-term contact with minerals, a phenomenon found in many rivers, and especially lakes. Fish from mineral-poor water are accustomed to very low ppm counts, and may indeed have evolved a need for such conditions. Of interest to potential barb breeders, eggs from soft water species often will not hatch in hard water.

Aquarium test kits do not measure all hardness, and we advise an advanced aquarist or fishbreeder to acquire an electronic meter to measure electrical conductivity, a more accurate measure of the minerals in water.

Filtration

Knowing what minerals are or are not in your water is the first step in understanding the water in your aquarium. Keeping that water as free as possible from pollution is the next step. How you maintain water quality will have a lot to do with your success.

Biological Filtration

There is more life in a healthy aquarium than meets the eye. While only the largest and most lightly populated aquariums have a chance of becoming reasonably functioning ecosystems, the attempt to manipulate nature's processes to our own ends is a big part of this hobby. It's not just your fish and plants that should be alive, but also your aquarium's filtration system. A biological filter is an artificially maintained ecosystem that should be viewed as a living "creature."

Biological filters make use of bacteria to minimize the negative effects of wastes on your closed system. A biological filter favors the growth of bacteria that consume toxic ammonia, a common by-product of aquatic life, converting it into less toxic nitrites. Other bacteria in the filter convert nitrites to even less dangerous nitrates. The most effective way to reduce nitrate levels is to do regular 25 percent water changes. Barbs love fresh, clean water, given that they are animals of flowing rivers.

There are two approaches to starting a filter. The traditional way is to start slowly, with very few fish, to give the beneficial bacteria present in your tank time to colonize the filter; this can take four to six weeks. During this time, your water quality will be unstable, and overstocking in a tank where fish are under such environmental stress is a quick ticket to an epidemic. You need some fish at the start to "feed" the filter, but too many and your new system will crash.

You can accelerate the process by adding gravel, plants, or other already bacterially colonized objects to the tank. Or, you can go with technology and purchase bacterial starter cultures at any good aquarium store. An efficient culture will rapidly jump-start your system.

The water test kits sold in aquarium stores can be useful for monitoring these early stages in the life of your filter, so that you can know when stocking levels can be increased.

Knowing how the collection of organisms we call a filter works is one thing, but you should also be aware of the great choice of efficient filtration machinery available to you. Which is best for you and your barbs? Biological filters come in several formats.

Outside Power Filters

These filters are probably the most popular option, as they are inexpensive, easy to find, and relatively efficient. Quality versions are also quiet, a serious consideration for family-room setups. They pull water from the tank into a box outside the tank, run it through a biological filter (usually a sponge) and, optionally, a chemical medium. The sponge or other biological medium doubles as a mechanical filter, which can be a drawback as it can become clogged and inefficient.

Most outside filters pour the water back with great force. This circulates heat and oxygen in the tank, and agitates the surface. Many barbs and danios will play in the oxygenated current, sometimes even swimming "upstream" into the filter. You may have to devise a system to keep your fish from either becoming trapped in the filter box or feeling obliged to jump to escape from the predicament this will get them into. Watching barbs play in the current from a safely set-up outside power filter can be a lot of fun.

Cannister filter: A variation on this theme is the popular cannister filter, which draws the water into a sealed cannister for mechanical, chemical, and biological filtration. These are highly efficient, but can be annoying to keep clean. Since they are sealed, it can also be hard to monitor their cleanliness.

Sponges or other biological filtration media should be rinsed in dechlorinated water when they show signs of clogging, as part of the routine maintenance of your tank. Remember,

Habitat of **Gastromyzon** *stone suckers in Malaysia.*

The "Scooter" (Barbucca diabolica) is a small loach with an easily-remembered name.

Loaches, like this Botia lochachata, *are excellent snail eaters.*

The Skunk Loach (Botia morleti) *is a characteristically shy aquarium fish.*

The common Indian Loach (Neomacheilus botia).

The albino Kuhli Loach (Pangio kuhlii) *is readily available throughout the aquarium hobby.*

your filter bacteria are living creatures that help you keep your fish healthy, and should be treated with respect. The chlorine or chloramine added to your municipal water to kill bacteria will do just that. Many hobbyists will draw some wastewater from the tank into a bucket, and rinse out the sponges in it.

Power filters can wreak havoc on many smaller floating and unrooted plants. The vegetation, in turn, will clog filter intakes. These filters work much better with rooted aquatic plants. They are also a disaster with barb fry. Lower-volume power filters can have a porous filtration sponge fitted on to the intake, as a small fish protecting prefilter.

Undergravel Filters

One of the oddest things about undergravel filters is their ability to cause debates among experienced aquarists. A new fishkeeper going from store to store seeking advice can receive completely contradictory opinions on this older technology. Undergravel filters are excellent biological filtration options, if they are well maintained and used properly. These filters, powered by either air pumps or very quiet powerhead underwater pumps, draw water through the tank bed, ideally of 2 inches (5 cm) or so of gravel. The bacteria in the gravel perform excellent biological filtration, but the gravel bed can very rapidly become clogged with debris and thereby lose its efficiency.

Undergravel filters should be used with regular gravel vacuuming, regular water changes, live plants, and light stocking. Especially when used with high-volume powerheads, they are excellent filters for barbs. They do not work well if the tank is too crowded, or if you overfeed your fish.

Air Pump–powered Filters

Sponge and box filters get minimal attention in aquarium literature, but they are very useful in specific applications. Sponge filtration provides biological filtration by drawing water through a bacteria-loaded sponge, via a suction created by rising air bubbles from a pump. They do clog with time. It is best to run two in a tank, so your cleaning of one sponge, which often temporarily drops the bacterial population, will not leave your fish unprotected. Plastic box filters are designed as air-driven mechanical filters—filtration systems that simply remove floating particles from water—but can be modified for biological filtration with sponge inserts, or a layer of small lava rocks or

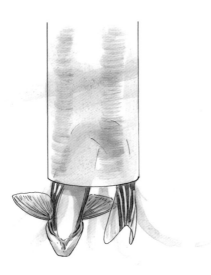

An unprotected hose can present a threat to fish.

A hose fitted with a strainer is safer for use around fish.

gravel on the bottom as a home for beneficial bacteria. Neither of these options provides the oxygen-loaded outflow levels so loved by most barbs. Given barbs' tendency to make a bit of a mess, these are not the most recommended filters for your fish, as they perform minimal mechanical filtration, and remove few sediments from the water. They are great for quarantine tanks, and for fry-raising systems.

Trickle filters are large and relatively expensive, but very efficient for both biological filtration and oxygenation. They are not often used for barbs, unless they are used as part of a central system with many aquariums connected to one filter via a plumbing system. These filters are beloved by do-it-yourself aquarists, who can find many plans for constructing these devices through mail-order sources or on the Internet, or who can amuse themselves for hours reinventing the wheel with these often homemade systems. They take up a lot of space, but do a fine job.

Fluidized bed filters are a recent innovation, but are not really necessary for keeping the standard barbs. For some of the delicate, rare species, it may be worth the higher cost to explore these expensive-to-maintain options, but light stocking, consistent water changes, and traditional filtration is a better option, at least for new aquarists.

Freshwater protein skimmers, based on a tried-and-true saltwater system, are a new and impressive option, but they are more for larger central filtration systems.

For fishkeepers with a taste for the "giant" species, like the popular tinfoil barb, high-end

filters are a good investment. The huge tanks these fish need work well with all of the advanced systems.

Mechanical Filtration

Mechanical filters are limited in their use. They make the water look good, but don't necessarily improve its quality. Their job is to remove solid sediments from water. They are best used along with biological filters, as their role is very much a cosmetic one.

There are several options on the market that offer chemical and mechanical packages in one filter.

Chemical Filtration

Chemical filters usually use charcoal or resins to remove elements from water. Again, they are best used in conjunction with biological systems. If you purchase a chemical filtration unit, be certain you will have a source of replacement filtration media.

AQUASCAPING

A barb aquarium gives free rein to the creativity of a fishkeeper. As long as your fish have clean, open water to swim in, they don't demand much. While other fish groups, such as the always popular cichlids, will demolish the décor of a tank that doesn't suit their individual plans, barbs let you do the planning, which allows you to view the aquarium as a garden space that can be made as beautiful as the fish inhabiting it.

Setting Up the Tank

How a tank is set up is very much a thing of fashion. The aquarium world has seen décors based on brightly colored plastics, sunken skeletons, bubbling fluorescent fixtures, rigidly researched natural aquascapes, brown, red, pink, purple, white, or black gravel, glow-in-the-dark plastic plants, all-natural vegetation, and everything in between. The motifs are simple enough, as they correspond to the tastes we have in our own homes and, especially for those with the space, our gardens. You can arrange your tank with the precise and carefully tended geometry usually reserved for bedding plants, or with the riotous growth of an English garden.

The Rosy Barb (Barbus conchonius) is deservedly among the most popular aquarium fish.

A good approach is to view your aquarium as a zoo space. Do you want your animals to pace in a bare cage, or do you want to try to emulate a natural environment as much as you can in your limited space? The phrasing of the question gives away the authors' prejudices. Here's how we'd approach barb setups for the average aquarium.

✔ Looked at from above, most aquariums are rectangles. You should first find a backing for your tank, as a well-chosen one will highlight the colors of your fish and plants while hiding the hang-on-the-back electrical equipment. Often, painting the back of the tank a dark color is the best option. Acrylic craft paints work well and offer a good range of colors.

✔ By using driftwood or stone, you can create terraces close to the back of the aquarium, to break up the monotony of a flat-bottom

Cave Fish

The dark world of water-filled caves is one habitat few aquarists will try to copy. In the aquarium hobby, the Mexican Blind Cave tetra (*Astyanax fasciatus mexicanus*) has a secure niche as a novelty fish. What works for a characin is bound to have been tried by a barb. There are no fewer than 30 Cypriniformes with populations living in the total or near total darkness of caves. None of them are aquarium fish, in spite of their being fascinating animals. Many are endangered species. All of these creatures have adaptations to heighten their nonvisual senses, even if not all have the totally atrophied eyes hobbyists might expect from cave fish.

surface. Driftwood can rise to the surface, an especially attractive option if you attach plants or aquatic moss to the wood.

✔ You can also use tall plants along the back. The traditional technique for setting up a tank is to use tall plants along the back, plants of medium height in the middle, and short, grassy types close to the front glass. This schema does not work in small tanks, but does serve as a solid starting point.

✔ Interesting effects can be achieved by using plants and other décor elements to break up the aquarist's line of vision within the tank. A line of tall plants can jut forward to the front glass, while half of the tank could be planted with mainly low-growing plants, to create variation in the depth of what you see. If your aquarium placement allows you to view your tank from the side, as well as through the front glass, there's no reason why you can't aquascape for both perspectives.

✔ While many fish groups will tunnel through the gravel, digging trenches and bringing down your carefully constructed terraces, small barbs let you decide how you want their home to look. If you avoid fine-leaved, edible plants, your fish will leave your tank to run as you wish it to.

Setups for Different Fish

Look closely at the barbs that have caught your interest. If they are high-bodied, and have flashy, silvery scales, you can be sure they survive by "hiding" in the open. Sunshine reflecting off silver is the perfect open-water camouflage. You can predict these fish will need a lot of room, and bright surface areas.

Zebra danios: Torpedo-shaped *Danio rerio* (zebra danios) demand a different setup. These are fish of fast-flowing, shallow streams. Their inability to resist running up a current shows this, as does their approach to cover. Their streams are open in the middle, with overhanging plants along the margins. Zebras like to scoot into the open water, but will rest under overhanging leaves, especially if the plants are close to the filter outflow. Long, low tanks are ideal for these animals.

Tiny barbs: Tiny barbs, such as the miniature *Rasbora, Sundadanio,* and *Boraras,* are neither silvery nor built for speed. Their deeper colors offer different information. A correct guess would put them into a darkened, heavily planted tank with a lot of shelter along the bottom. These richly colored fish are often found in the leaf litter along the bottom of

Choosing Tankmates for Your Barbs

Far too often, aquarium-keepers define compatibility in terms of behavior. With barbs and their relatives, aggressiveness is an important factor. Many Barbus species are naturally inclined to nip at the fins of other fish in their vicinity, while Rasboras often becomes a nipping victim. The Cichlid that makes an ideal companion for Rosy Barbs will easily demolish a delicate Rasbora, and happily munch on tiny Boraras. With a family this large, there are no hard and fast rules regarding behavior patterns.

Luckily, there are effective approaches that can be used in dealing with compatibility problems. When you stock an aquarium, you must research each individual species and its needs before you buy. For example, if your fish of choice are active, flowing water fish like Danios, then a tankmate from a habitat of slow-moving, oxygen-poor water will not adapt well to either the conditions you offer, or the active behavior of the Danios it will live with.

Water chemistry is also important. *Barbus rhomboocellatus* is a beautiful rarity from blackwater conditions. It thrives in acidic, mineral-poor water. Keep it with a hardwater fish like, for example, most livebearers, and an outbreak of velvet (Oodinium) is almost guaranteed.

Many barbs are very comfortable in an unheated aquarium. A cool water barb kept with warm water tetras will lead a shortened, often lethargic life, as will Amazonian tetras if kept under conditions suited to many barbs.

Indeed, even within the loosely defined barb group, there are extremes. If you attempt to keep the often-expensive Asian rummy nose, *Sawbwa resplendens*, in a tank with blackwater barbs, the result will be disastrous. If you make the appropriate preparations by studying the fish first, you will learn that *Sawbwa* are hardwater fish that will do best when kept with companions, barbs or otherwise, with the same environmental needs. Keeping an aquarium is a reader's hobby, and knowledge of your fish and their needs are essential before you make any purchases.

jungle swamps, streams, and pools. Nothing that small could survive in the conditions favored by larger barbs in the wild, so we should not expect them to prosper under such conditions in captivity. Give them lots of hiding places and floating plants and you will discover they don't need to hide when they feel secure.

Loaches: Loaches are another challenge, as many are active once the lights go off. Their flattened bellies speak of a need to sit on the bottom, while their frenetic activity levels clearly call for oxygenated, clean, and flowing water. Provide them with the proper aquarium, and they will provide you with loach behavior at its best.

PLANTS

An underwater green thumb can take time and effort to develop, and this aspect of the hobby can be discouraging for many. Choosing your plants as carefully as you choose your fish is important. With one of the many aquatic plant fertilizers on the market, and adequate lighting, the rudiments of this aspect of aquarium keeping should become easy to master.

The quest for quality plants should be taken as seriously as the search for healthy fish. Not all the species listed here will be available in every market, although the expansion of the Internet, and mail-order companies is making it increasingly easier to track down rarities. In this manual, we will concentrate on plants that are easy to grow and maintain. We will avoid fine-leafed species, which are generally eaten by barbs, and concentrate on the basic species that should offer a good chance of success. In reading this, remember, whatever your choice, you are always better off buying plants you have seen. This brings us to the need to establish a good relationship with a quality local retailer.

top: Male White Cloud Mountain minnows in typical display posture.
bottom: The Tiger Danio is threatened in nature.

Types of Plants

Tall Substrate Plants

There are several aspects to be studied before choosing substrate plants. You must consider how tall the plant grows (determining where in the tank you will plant), what water conditions are needed, and, most important, the light requirements of the species.

Vallisneria americana var. gigantea: This tall grasslike plant needs moderate light. It is for the deep tank. Its leaves will trail over the surface, and look especially good in a tank with a current. *Vallisneria americana* leaves are very tough and sturdy, and therefore barb resistant.

Vallisneria tortifolia: This is a smaller aquatic grass that under good conditions will spread quickly. It needs moderate light, a fact that makes it a good fit for the beginner's tank. Even in dim light, it will most likely survive, if not prosper. It is excellent at the back of a standard-sized aquarium. Its spread (through runners) may have to be controlled, as it will rapidly fill in many of the areas you create as open swimming spaces if you have bottom-oriented species in a community tank.

Sagittaria subulata: This is a medium light grassy plant. There is a related dwarf species, *S. pusilla*, that grows to 4 inches (10 cm) and will spread along the foreground. *S. subulata* will reach 24 inches (60 cm).

Bacopa spp. (caroliniana or **monnieri):** *Bacopa* is good for a well-lit tank with a space between the cover and the water. These stalky, round-leaved North American plants will produce small but elegant flowers at the water surface. They have a tendency to lose the leaves at their base as they grow taller. Trimming is necessary if these plants are to maintain their beauty; however, on a positive note, their tough leaves are rarely trimmed by hungry plant-eating barbs.

Hygrophilia difformis: This is an excellent candidate for people who feel they can't grow aquarium plants. It can float or be rooted. It doesn't like mineral-poor water, which makes it great for most municipal systems. *Hygrophilia* will either grow rapidly for you, or not at all. If an aquarist is successful with this usually easy plant, the tank will be overrun without regular removal of excess plants.

Hygrophilia polysperma: This plant roots and grows quickly under moderate light. It needs trimming, or it will take on a decidedly palm tree-like shape, losing its leaves closer to the bottom. The related *H. corymbosa* is a little more difficult, especially in its light-loving red forms. The latter are not suggested for beginners.

Ludwigia repens: This is a plant with a need for bright light. It is often available, and beginners usually can't resist giving it a try. It is not an easy subject unless your tank is extremely well illuminated.

Rotala spp. (macrandra or **rotundifolia):** This pretty plant is generally available as cuttings. If they take root in your tank, they are lovely plants; however, they do best under moderately bright light. If you add light capacity to a commercially available hood, you can do well with this one, but it probably won't take under the standard single fluorescent bulb.

Medium-height Substrate Plants

These plants will rarely get to the surface in the average tank, and are therefore excellent as foreground vegetation. They are also good options as background plants for smaller or shallow tanks.

Cryptocoryne spp.: "Crypts," as they are commonly called, are superb plants. Many aquarists avoid trying them, as these rooted plants tend to be more expensive than anchored together cuttings. This can be a false economy as, while cuttings often don't take root and need to be replaced, cryptocorynes can take off and prosper rapidly under even dim lighting. They aren't plants for the aquarist who needs answers, as they are often misidentified in pet shops. Unless you are in contact with an aquatic plant specialist or nursery, which crypt you have may always remain a mystery to you.

All plants will grow for some people, and not for others, but with crypts, your chances of success are very good. They prosper in soft and acid water, and will grow slowly and steadily under the fairly dim light found on the bottom of most planted tanks, even under moderately alkaline conditions. Put into medium-bright light, these often reddish plants spread rapidly along the bottom of the tank via runners. Crypts will sometimes even form carpets along the bottom, a very attractive sight.

The main practical differences between crypt species is size—some will reach 20 inches (50 cm) plus, while others stay very small at 4 inches (10 cm). It is best to consult with your plant dealer, or check a quality plant book, prior to buying. You may have trouble deciding exactly which crypt you have, but the general type is easy to guess at.

Cryptocorynes are Asian plants, which means that in nature, they are found in the company of many popular barbs.

Echinodorus spp. (Amazon swords): Amazon swords also come in a bewildering range of species and sizes, and can be seen as South America's answer to the crypt. Most need medium to bright light, and do best with fertilization. The most attractive versions are centerpiece plants for the decorated aquarium. When happy, they spread quickly.

Hydrocotyle leucocephala: Water pennywort produces round, lily pad-like leaves, which may be nibbled by some barbs. They need light, but this is less of a problem as the leaves grow to the surface. This plant will also try to leave the tank, and can spread right across the tank hood if left to run. Specimens on top of your tank cover make for an unexpected display, but the submerged sections lose their lovely leaves.

Aponogeton spp.: *Aponogeton* are bulb plants, with varying periods of dormancy. *Aponogeton crispus* are the best option for most aquariums. Bulbs from this family often show up in unlikely sources, in the garden sections of department stores as well as in small pet shops.

Ceratopteris thalictroides: Water sprite is a commonly available, easily grown medium-light plant. It is an excellent organic filter for toxic substances in the fish tank. Barbs can nibble at the soft leaves, but the growth rate of the plants is such that it is not usually a problem.

Nymphaea spp.: These bulb plants are excellent candidates for medium-light tanks. The surface leaves feed the growth of the bulb, but may overly shade the tank. Trimming is a necessity. In a deep tank, they look surprisingly good if placed at the front close to the glass. Barbs look wonderful as they swim through the stalky, lily pad-topped stems of *Nymphaea*.

Epiphytic (Rhizome-rooted) Plants

These low-light, easy to grow plants are highly recommended. They produce tough leaves and root structures that cannot be buried, but rather, should be tied onto rocks or driftwood. Buried rhizomes rot, but tied-on structures will attach to their hosts.

Bolbitis heudelotii: This attractive African fern spreads well under low to moderate light, with a slight current. It can be hard to find and pricey, but is worth trying. It grows slowly, and may need to be cleaned if you have a lot of algae in your tank. These plants can live and prosper indefinitely, under good conditions, spreading slowly but steadily.

Anubias spp.: There are a number of attractive African *Anubias* species. These slow growers do well under dim light, and will grow steadily under brighter conditions. *Anubias barteri* variety nana, the dwarf *Anubias,* is

A second form of Barbus denisonii, *showing more red in the dorsal fin than seen in the nominate species.*

Rasbora dusonensis *is one of many similar species.*

This is one of many newly introduced barbs from India, probably a Neolissocheilus species.

The Signal Rasbora (Rasbora dorsioccelata) *is a jaunty, hardy, little community fish.*

Choosing Plants

How much light you have to offer your plants will determine your success in making them thrive. For the sake of simplicity, we will look at aquarium lighting as either:

Low to moderate: one fluorescent tube, or an incandescent fixture, per 20 gallons;

Medium to strong: two fluorescent tubes per 30 gallons;

Bright: multiple fluorescent tubes, or a high-tech lighting system.

This isn't a precise system, as aquariums vary. One tube on a shallow tank will provide as much light as two on a very deep aquarium. Some improvisation and experimentation will always be necessary. Remember too that a plant that can survive and even grow slowly under low light conditions can flourish under stronger lighting.

Plants for the low to moderate light system:
- ✔ *Vallisneria tortifolia*
- ✔ *Hygrophilia difformis*
- ✔ *Hygrophilia polysperma*
- ✔ *Cryptocoryne* sp.
- ✔ *Bolbitis heudelotii*
- ✔ *Anubias* sp.
- ✔ *Microsorum pteropus*
- ✔ *Vesicularia dubyana*

Plants for the medium to strong light system:
- ✔ *Vallisneria americana* var. *gigantea*
- ✔ *Sagittaria subulata*
- ✔ *Bacopa* sp.
- ✔ *Echinodorus* sp.
- ✔ *Aponogeton* sp.
- ✔ *Ceratopteris thalictroides*
- ✔ *Nymphaea* sp.
- ✔ *Ceratophyllum demersum*
- ✔ *Hydrocotyle leucocephala*

Plants for the bright light system:
- ✔ *Ludwigia repens*
- ✔ *Rotala* sp.

the most common form in aquariums. Other extremely rare species will sometimes show up in unlikely places, especially if you have a local importer who brings in African barbs.

Microsorum pteropus (Java Fern): This is the plant for people who can't grow plants. Java fern is a beautiful plant that is incredibly easy to keep. Tied to a proper substrate under moderate lighting, it will spread steadily. Its long, elegant, bright leaves provide an excellent backdrop. Don't despair if the pricey plant you buy disappears; *Microsorum* have been known to reappear in tanks months after they seemed to have died.

Vesicularia dubyana (Java Moss): Java moss can be attached to driftwood or rocks. It is an attractive, dim-light plant that will grow almost anywhere. Barbs love to spawn in it, and fry will sometimes survive under a rich carpet of Java moss. Beware though, as it will choke the intakes of power filters.

Floating Rootless Plants

Floating plants are not a necessity in an average barb aquarium. For the keeper of open-water, active schooling barbs, light is a must, and floating plants will block illumination as they spread. Where they come in more than handy is with the shy, usually slender-bodied rain forest species. Cherry barbs, *Rasbora,* or many of the smaller African *Barbus* species will develop excellent colors if they can move from shade to light. They are also quite useful in breeding tanks.

Rootless floating plants also draw nutrition from the aquarium's water, a process quite helpful for the maintenance of good conditions. Many aquarists keep them in barb tanks for this purpose alone. The most common floating plant for barb tanks is *Ceratophyllum demersum* (Hornwort). It is a brittle-leaved plant that barbs will not eat, as they will other floaters. It will grow rapidly under good surface lighting; however, if unhappy, it will dissolve and pollute your tank just as quickly. Once established, it is hardy. For many newcomers to the hobby, it seems to be the only plant that will grow, as once it survives its initial acclimation, it thrives.

Plastic Plants

Plastic plants can be snob magnets, and many aquarists view them as the height of bad taste. That being said, not everyone can successfully grow live plants, especially if their source of water offers extremes. There is a place for plastic plants, as the more realistic options among them are very convincing, and very attractive; however, plastic plants serve no biological function, and at best are merely a substitute for the real thing.

FEEDING YOUR BARBS

Feeding fish is fun, and is the point in the day when we pay the most attention to our barbs. For us as well as our fish, a regular feeding routine is necessary.

Overfeeding

Many barbs will remind you if they get hungry by charging the glass as you approach or, in some cases, energetically splashing or even jumping. The problem is usually not forgetting to feed your fish, but rather, giving in and overfeeding them. Kindness is a great killer of aquarium fish. Many popular barbs are prone to obesity, and indeed seem to aspire to it. Extra weight seriously shortens their lives, and can lead to sterility, and overfeeding increases the amount of waste (uneaten food and excrement) in the tank, taxing your filtration and water quality, and increasing the likelihood of disease.

Types of Food

Most barbs aren't picky eaters. They will eat anything and everything they can fit in their mouths. In general, their food should contain some vegetable content, but standard

*The variable, beautiful Fire Barb is really a rasbora (**R. vaterifloris**).*

aquarium trade staple foods are good as the core of the diet. If you use flake or pellet food, you should alternate several types, just for variety. It is better to avoid bulk purchases, as once opened, flake food loses vitamins quickly.

Color Food

Most flake food manufacturers offer color-enhancing food as part of their general product line. If your barbs have red or orange in their coloration, they seem to often react strongly and positively to such foods. Color food should never be a staple, but can be a good supplement.

Live Foods

Most aquarists have easy access to a range of flake foods; live foods are a different question. While many aquarists consider it disturbing to use live animals as food for their fish, they are part of the natural diet of aquarium fish. Small insects and crustaceans can be fed frozen, but in their live form they are more nutritious, and stimulate natural behavior in fish. Many newly imported, rare wild fish need to be weaned onto flake through a gradual shift from small live food animals to the more easily-used commercial options. Species not inclined to scavenge can take time to recognize inert flake as a food item.

In large centers, aquarium stores will offer a range of "short-term" live foods. Small bags of adult brine shrimp can be hard to keep alive for any period of time, and should be fed quickly. The same is true for the popular black-worms found in many pet shops. These animals need to be kept in flowing water or they will rapidly become a source of bacterial disease. A better option is to cultivate your own live foods as a supplement to a flake-based diet, or to avoid the problem altogether, since most barbs aren't picky.

Brine shrimp: The live food that is easiest to raise is freshly hatched brine shrimp. If you can acquire quality eggs, hatch rates should be excellent. The tiny brine shrimp should be hatched in aerated salt water. The containers used will vary, and reusable and easy-to-clean hatcheries can be purchased or made. You can easily find special fine-mesh nets for collecting the small, color-rich food animals, which are ideal for raising young barbs. It is much more difficult to offer recipes for salinity in the hatch water than it used to be. The same is true for temperature. At one point, most of the eggs (really cysts) sold came from two sources, the Great Salt Lake in Utah and San Francisco Bay in the United States; however, several years of bad harvests opened the door for commercial collection of eggs of different but equally useful species from Tibet, Central Asia, and Russia. Check with your dealer for the amount of salt needed for the type you buy, as it can vary considerably.

Whiteworms: You can also culture white-worms (you can find cultures at aquarium clubs, on the Internet, or in some aquarium stores), on dark, cool soil on a diet of soaked dried cat food, or wingless fruit flies, a labora-tory animal.

Insects: Many hobbyists enjoy collecting their own live food. *Daphnia* (water fleas); var-ious types of small aquatic insects; and mos-quito larvae head the list. In many areas, the risk of mosquito-borne disease makes cultiva-tion of mosquito larvae illegal, but collected with a net and fed to your fish before they can develop into biters—an important considera-tion!—this natural food is great for triggering spawning behavior in barbs. If you find a likely pond and decide to collect your own food, take some time to sit down with an insect field guide and become familiar with all the preda-tory water bugs, especially dragonfly larvae, as they do pose a danger to small barbs. Some aquarists will keep screened *Daphnia* cultures in a shady part of the yard, especially if they want to stimulate breeding by uncooperative species.

Frozen Food

You may also choose to ignore live food altogether, and opt for frozen fish food. Adding frozen bloodworms, mosquito larvae, *Cyclops,* glassworms, or brine shrimp to your barbs' diets will accelerate growth and quickly increase the brightness of their colors.

The most economical and available frozen food, bloodworms (really bright red, wormlike midge larvae) are a great value, but are also very dangerous to many allergy sufferers. They seem to affect people who are allergic to dust mites, and can cause serious reactions, even if touched. In their freeze-dried form they can be extremely hazardous to asthma sufferers, and should be avoided by any fishkeeper with a history of allergies. Frozen adult brine shrimp are less valuable as food, but safer for the allergic.

Caution: Never use frozen food that has been thawed and refrozen.

How Much and How Often to Feed

Whatever you use, feed sparingly, giving what your fish will eat in a few minutes, once or ideally, twice a day. Frequent (two to three times per day) feedings of small quantities are suggested for young barbs. Older fish should not eat more than twice daily, and even once a day is adequate. Your barbs, especially if you keep the popular *Barbus* species, will beg shamelessly and effectively, but don't give in.

Vacations

Vacation time can be stressful for the concerned fishkeeper, but is not a major problem for the fish.

✔ Clean your tank a few days before you leave, and make certain your equipment is in top shape.

✔ Try to find a friend who will check in on temperatures, top up summertime evaporation, and remove any dead fish.

✔ Don't worry about feeding healthy adult fish unless you plan to be gone for more than a week. Your barbs will be fine without food for such a period. If you go for longer, your fish buddy should be supplied with prepared portions of food, unless he or she is an experienced aquarist. Clearly explain how little food your fish really need.

✔ The number one cause of barb death during vacations is inexperienced feeders who fall for the begging routines of a school of enthusiastic fish, and pollute the tank.

HEALTH AND FITNESS

It may look absurd to mention "fitness" in a fish-health chapter, but with barbs, prevention is the key to health. No aspect of the aquarium fish hobby discourages more new aquarists than the death of their new fish, and yet, fish diseases should not be a problem in the average tank.

The Retailer

You must start with good healthy fish. The most important step is to find a retailer you can trust.

✔ Look for a clean, well-lit store where the fish are kept in large enough tanks and low population densities.

✔ Check to see if the owner or employees are open to answering questions, and seem to know a lot about the animals they sell. Helpful people at your local shop will greatly simplify your fishkeeping experience, and will go out of their way to make certain a loyal customer is a well-informed one.

✔ In analyzing a store, remember that not all aspects of fish health are easily controlled by the staff.

Your Future Barbs' Journey

Your future barbs probably started out their lives in either an Asian or Floridian fish farm,

The Maharadja Barb (**Barbus sajadrensis**).

where they are bred in huge quantities, and raised under conditions that favor both growth and epidemics. Crowding is part of the business, as is the use of antibiotics to deal with its consequences. The next stage in your future fishes' journey can be a long one, as tightly packed in very little water, they are flown to a wholesaler. They may barely be acclimated to their new surrounding before they are on the move again, to the store where you get to see them. For the fish, this is a stressful process. A good retailer will choose sources of fish carefully, but while the system functions extremely well, with significantly less fish mortality than we might expect, newly imported fish are fragile.

What Look for in New Barbs

Luckily, at least for the fishkeeper, the signs of such stress are easily observed.

✔ Look for the shape of the barbs that interest you. Their fins should be carried erect, and should not be ragged.

✔ Barbs will nip at each other when they are overcrowded, but avoid tanks in which fish show visible damage.

✔ The weight of the fish should be evenly distributed, and the belly should not be too sunken. Newly imported fish will be thinner than established specimens, as distributors will not feed them for several days prior to sending them out, so they have fewer wastes to foul their shipping water.

✔ If the fish you want are newly imported, watch them feed. A fish made thin by a disease or parasite will lose its appetite, while a tankful of hungry barbs will surprise you with their voracity. Barbs that do not want to eat are not a natural phenomenon.

✔ Look at the eyes of the fish. Are they clear? Cloudiness or milkiness is a serious warning sign.

✔ Inspect the flanks for scale damage, or for protruding scales, a symptom of internal infection.

✔ Look for milky patches or fungus on the skin.

✔ Check for white spots or cysts on the body or fins. This is a sign of one of two rapidly spreading parasites, ich or oodinium.

✔ Check for whiteness around the lips.

✔ Watch to see if the fish scratches itself against objects in the aquarium.

✔ Stand back and look at the tank. Are there any dead fish, or any emaciated or deformed individuals in it? Deformities can be a symptom of fish tuberculosis. If the answer is yes, move on. Never buy a seemingly healthy individual from a tank with sick individuals, as the stresses of shipping and pet shop life leave all fish open to attack.

✔ If you observe an easily identifiable disease in a tank, ask whether the fish are for sale. Remember that knowledge is half of this hobby, and that in a low-quality outlet, employees may not know any more about fish and their diseases than a newcomer to the hobby will. At the same time, this is a hobby that attracts people who enjoy learning, and in larger centers, good stores with their customers' interests at heart should have no trouble finding staff qualified by their curiosity about fish and their own reading and experience as hobbyists. The store that offers the best customer support and information may not be the cheapest, but it will save you trouble and offer you services a nonspecialized store can't. No responsible retailer wants to risk losing customers by selling sick fish to them, and no hobbyist wants to buy from a store that isn't concerned about its customers.

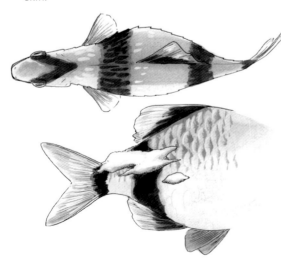

top: Bloat.

bottom: Fungus.

When You Are Ready to Buy

Assuming you have found a reliable store, and a tankful of healthy looking fish, you have two avenues open to you. Both involve that rarest of attributes—patience.

Quarantine

If you buy a group of barbs (for most species, six individuals is a good number), all sources say you should have a quarantine tank waiting for them. It should be a clean, bare tank, heated, filtered, and in a place where it can be observed. A couple of weeks of quarantine will give you time to watch for any developing parasites or infections.

There is no more sensible advice, but frankly, hardly anyone follows it. The "addictive" nature of this hobby is such that very few people can have a completely equipped tank sitting empty without turning it into yet another community setup.

The inability to quarantine is behind most epidemics in fish tanks. If you choose to take the risk of introducing diseases into your community, you can, to a degree, use your dealer's tanks for observation. This time-consuming approach means returning to the shop several times over a week, to observe the health of the fish. It also helps to have an "insider," which brings us back to the customer/retailer relationship. Most aquarium store employees will help a loyal customer by reporting on mortality in a new shipment, as well as on problems they have treated. Quarantine is always the best policy, but observation and

information can lessen risks to your established community considerably.

Making Sure Your Fish Stay Healthy

Even under what seem to be the best conditions, barbs can get sick. Unless the fish are very old, it may be the result of equipment of maintenance routine breakdowns.

Water: The best way to ensure that your fish will stay healthy is to keep the water clean, and within the parameters ideal for the species you are keeping. For example, fish from warm tropical climates easily get sick in cooler water. An outbreak of an opportunistic parasite can come from a chilling, from dirty water, or even from a water change where temperatures were not monitored. Water changes can lessen stress on the fish, reduce bacterial levels, and are the most important factor in keeping your fish healthy.

Medication: If you do have to medicate fish, remember that activated carbon and some chemical filtration resins will quickly remove medications from the aquarium water, so they

Fin rot.

top left: **Labeo victorianus** *comes from Lake Victoria.*

middle left: **Juvenile Garra (Garra dembeensis)** *are very difficult to properly identify.*

bottom left: **A Giant Humpheaded Barb (Neolissocheilus stracheyi)** *from the Mekong Delta.*

top right: **The Blue Botia (Botia Lecontei)** *can become aggressive as it ages.*

bottom right: **Juvenile Barbus arulius** *specimens do not show the spectacular finnage typical of adults.*

top: **Barbus denisonii** *is distinguished by the intense crimson streak at the front of its body. A native of India, it is more familiarly known as the Red Flash Shark.*
above: **Barbus rhombocellatus** *are normally shy and thrive in soft water.*
middle right: All Botia species have a spine under the eye which serves as a formidable weapon.
bottom right: To avoid injury from the spine, Botia must always be handled very carefully.

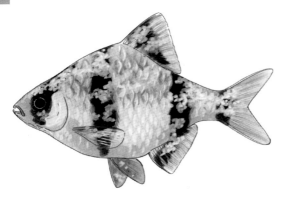

Oodinium.

must be removed and discarded; by returning the cartridge you may reintroduce the problem after you have cured the fish.

Here is a quick overview of some of the most commonly encountered diseases, and their treatments.

Common Diseases

Velvet—Oodinium

Velvet is caused by the tiny single-celled parasite called *Piscinoodinium pillulare*. This creature can remain dormant in an aquarium for quite some time, and will become evident only when deteriorating conditions weaken its targets' immune systems. When this happens, thousands of these parasites will settle on the fish and cause tiny white or yellowish spots, as if the fish were covered with a thin film of velvet or powdered sugar. Sometimes the infection will be limited to the gills where it will cause the fish to frequently scratch on the bottom or decorations, swim with clamped fins, or rock back and forth using only its pectorals. In some

cases, oodinium will become established on one or two individual fish, seemingly doing them very little harm. Don't count on this, though, as the parasite is generally fatal if untreated. It is especially deadly if it hits newly hatched fry.

Many preparations are available for this disease at your pet store; best are copper-based medications. Note that copper is extremely toxic at pH under 7, and always harmful to snails and other invertebrates. If the disease catches you unprepared and you cannot get to a store to purchase a commercial treatment, the addition of noniodized salt will help (one teaspoon per gallon), as will turning off the lights. Oodinium thrives in bright conditions.

Velvet is especially problematic with *Rasboras* and small rain forest barb types.

White Spot—Ichtyophthirius (Ich)

Ich is the number one killer of aquarium fish and without fail will attack every aquarist's fish at least once. This small protozoan parasite will show up as small white spots on the skin, fins, and eyes of the fish. It can be similar to oodinium, although it is generally larger and never yellowish. There are a number of forms of ich, which can vary in the damage they do to your fish. Treatment is fortunately easy if the infestation is diagnosed early. Always have enough medication on hand to treat your fish. Pet stores sell a large number of brands, and all of them work. Preparations that contain formalin or formaldehyde or the very effective medicinal dye malachite green should be handled with care due to their carcinogenic properties. Read the list of ingredients on the medication you are considering, and try to steer clear of these chemicals. There are many medications on the market that are safer to use.

Ich tends to strike when you have neglected your fish, or by Murphy's Law, when you do not have medication on hand. A good approach to save your fish when you don't have access to commercial treatments is to increase the temperature of the tank to 85°F (30°C), while making sure the water is clean. If you change water, be careful, as the parasite can spread quickly on equipment if you have more than one aquarium. Warm water accelerates the parasite's life cycle, and can kill free-swimming protozoans before they can latch onto their hosts. Old-time aquarists added salt, as with oodinium, to increase the protective slime coat on their fish. Like oodinium, ich seems to like light, so a few days of darkness can help. Methylene blue, an old-fashioned mouthwash ingredient available in both pet shops and pharmacies, can be added to darken the water. It is effective against ich.

All barbs and their relatives are affected by ich, although *Barbus* seem especially prone. With sensitive loaches, seek experienced advice before using a medication.

Bacterial Diseases

Bacterial diseases can easily break out if the water conditions are less than ideal. Other causes are buying infected or damaged fish, having fish injured by fighting, or older fish being kept in dirty water. The symptoms can include red sores on fins, body, or eyes of the fish, bloating, protruding eyes, or extreme listlessness. Treatment is usually with antibacterial drugs, which are becoming increasingly difficult to find. Some, such as tetracycline, have become ineffective because bacteria are now resistant. Check with your local store to see what drugs are available.

Ich.

Many jurisdictions have banned fish antibiotics without a veterinary prescription. A new alternative appearing on the market is medication based on tea tree or Asian "wild almond," "magic almond," or "almond tree" leaves, which do seem to have effective antibacterial properties for fish.

Fungus—Saprolegnia and Others

Fungus is in every aquarium, but is really a secondary disease that affects fish that have external injuries or are weakened by other diseases. Make sure that you have clean water and that there are no damaged or bullied fish in the aquarium. Fungus can appear as tufts, fine hairs, or slime on the fins, eyes, or body of infected fish. Often, removing the source of the injuries can stop the disease from spreading further. Physically removing the fungus tufts from the fish and placing the fish in a hospital aquarium with clean water helps, as can a salt bath; place 15 grams of noniodized kitchen salt in one liter of water and bathe affected fish for 10 minutes.

TB—Mycobacterium (Fish Tuberculosis)

The blind **Garra barreimiae barreimiae** *from Oman.*

Unfortunately, TB is becoming more common and can be found in both wild-caught and captive-raised fish. Barbs can be struck by this chronic disease, for which there is no cure. Symptoms include open sores or swelling on the body, deformities, swollen abdomens or foreheads, and scales "sticking out." Infected fish should be quickly and humanely euthanized. Fish TB can infect wounds and open sores on humans, where it can cause ridged knots or small sores. The rare but painful and slow-to-cure disease transmission is known to doctors as fish tank or swimming pool granuloma. An infection of healthy people is uncommon, but immunodefficient—or healthily cautious—people should wear gloves to handle fish or equipment around the aquarium.

Precautions

Whatever illness has hit your tank, certain precautions can keep it from returning. All equipment that has been in contact with sick or dying fish should be sterilized, for which we suggest the use of common household bleach. Filters, heaters, gravel, and inorganic ornaments can be sterilized by placing them in a covered bucket of water that has one-half cup of bleach added. To clean the tank itself, the same solution can be used. All items that have been in contact with bleach must be rinsed thoroughly and could also be placed outside to dry, to evaporate any remaining bleach.

Disease will always be a minor danger in well-cared-for aquariums. Prevention is the key, which brings us around to the early emphasis on fitness. Barbs need room to exercise, which we can provide by choosing a large enough tank and not crowding it. They need clean water and good food.

Under the correct conditions, many barb species will breed readily in the aquarium. In this sequence, a pair of Fire Barbs exhibit typical mating and territorial display behavior.

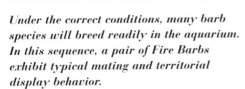

HOW-TO: BREEDING BARBS

Fish breeding can become an engrossing part of the hobby. At a certain point in their enjoyment of keeping their favorite species, aquarists may become curious about the biology of barbs, or may simply want to try something different. Some can find themselves keeping a rarely imported gem they want to enjoy for more than one relatively short generation.

For most species, begin with a healthy pair, although for others, a small group is suggested. All female fish chosen for breeding should be round-bellied from eggs, and all males alert and active. If you have the space, the sexes should be kept apart for a short period while they are receiving an excellent diet, ideally with a large portion of live or frozen foods. With some species, it is best to allow the fish to pair off on their own, as putting a male and female together will not guarantee spawning.

How you prepare your breeding tank will take experimentation. Barb eggs are adhesive, and in nature generally stick to underwater plants. Most aquarist-breeders will set up a shallow tank offering an ample amount of swimming space along with plenty of the fine-leaved (edible) plants we don't usually keep in barb community tanks. The water should be clean, but ideally aged and slightly acidic.

The pair is introduced to the tank in the evening, and the aquarium is situated so it will receive the morning sunlight. If all goes well, the fish will spawn (a quick, active affair, often involving wild swimming and even splashing) with the first light. Given the energy involved in the spawning act, your barbs will often be hungry afterward. Failure to remove the parents quickly will result in the eggs being eaten.

Many aquarists will use a structure known as a spawning grate with egg scattering barbs. Any easily sterilized plastic screening, with holes large enough to allow eggs to fall through, can be cut to fit the bottom of the tank. An older trick is to cover the bottom of the tank with several layers of sterilized glass marbles. Both approaches allow the hobbyist to view eggs that have fallen into areas the hungry parents can't reach.

Once the adult pair is back in its regular tank, swimming with the school and being conditioned for the next attempt, the aquarist will eagerly await the hatching of the fry. Often, a water change (at an equal temperature!) is in order, as males of some species produce enough extra sperm to foul the water in a small tank. Most barb eggs are not light-sensitive in the manner of the popular aquarium characin (tetra) species, but shading doesn't hurt. The eggs of blackwater rainforest fish like the Rasbora are light-

Typical barb spawning behavior.

It is not unusual for barbs to eat their eggs.

sensitive, so the back and sides of the spawning tank can be lined with newspaper.

Feeding the fry can be problematic, especially for species that produce huge numbers. Only attempt to raise as many fry as you feel you can successfully care for, as being overly ambitious will probably cost you an entire brood. With water changes and the proper attention, they will grow quickly. Most barb fry can be started on microorganisms, cultivated from cultures acquired from an aquarium club or from the Internet. Greenwater (standing water colored by a thick culture of suspended algae) is useful, if you can cultivate it on a windowsill. As well, the increasing popularity of Australasian rainbowfish, which have tiny fry, has led to an explosion of choices in dried microfoods, as the technology of the aquaculture industry makes its way into the home aquarium world. A reliable local pet shop should be able to point you to some excellent egg-layer fry foods. Once your baby barbs are big enough, freshly hatched brine shrimp can be added as a growth food par excellence.

In large, lightly stocked, and heavily planted tanks, or with popular species like *Tanichthys albonubes*, the White Mountain Cloud Minnow, or *Danio rerio*, the Zebra Danio, fry will some-times appear in a single species tank and grow up with the parents. A community of either fish, with no predators added, can run itself for years. A "species tank" stocked only with White Mountain Clouds actually makes a very beauti-ful spectacle.

While it is extremely easy to coax some barbs into spawning, others are great challenges for aquarists who take pleasure in breeding their fish. Many of the Loaches have not been bred in captivity, although the use of hormone

Marbles at the bottom of a barb spawning tank protect fry from their normally hungry parents.

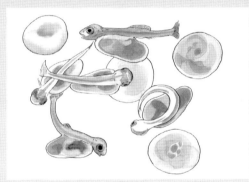

Barb eggs hatching.

injections has produced eggs from some on large, commercial fish farms. So too, many of the delicate blackwater barbs have not been bred, although this may be based more on their rarity than on their difficulty. There remains a great deal of ground to be broken on the barb breeding front, and there are a number of species with which an ambitious hobbyist can become the first person to view their reproduc-tive activity and successfully raise fry.

The barbs constitute a variety of interesting genera. Some species are familiar; others are quite rare. The following descriptions of many barb species also provide guidance for keeping and understanding them.

Asian Barbus Species

Any exploration of aquarium barbs has to focus on Asian *Barbus* first. These are the most commonly encountered barbs in the aquarium trade, in a genus so large and diverse it is unlikely that it will stand the long term test of scientific study. The problem lies in the diversity of the group, with heavyweight European food fish in the same genus as diminutive African and Asian species. The idea of organizing species into genera is to clarify their relationships, and *Barbus* currently resembles a very confusing taxonomic desk drawer. Many of these fish should end up in new genera, once scientists shine a light on them. In investigating further, the curious aquarist will already find a lot of confusion in the naming of these fish. Past attempts to classify them by looking at their barbels may have given us genus names such as *Puntius* in some literature, but the fish themselves proved impossible to keep in the new systems devised. Within species, the characteristics chosen for definition can vary wildly.

Barbus nigrofasciatus, *the Ruby Barb.*

In one area, a given fish may have barbels, while its neighbors of the same species don't. It seems *Barbus* as a category is too vast to help us, but it is also very challenging to define the break-off points for the creation of new genera. For now, we will accept them as one big happy family, and look at them as aquarium fish.

And as aquarium fish, they are magnificent. These fish swim throughout the aquarium, schooling at all levels in a constant reexploration of their homes. A quick look at their usual habitats in the wild shows why this is so. Our aquarium fish are relatively small, in regions where large predators are many. While they are fish of river systems, their actual homes are on the margins of great rivers. In the dry season, they inhabit small streams and ponds, or sidearms of larger bodies of water. They favor places offering cover, but also swimming room. One of their main protections is their life in the shallows. Often, the bottom is rich with decaying plant matter, while terrestrial plants trail onto the water. *Barbus* generally will root through any mulm or fine sand on the bottom of a fish tank.

The rainy season is what has produced the adaptability that makes barbs the perfect aquarium fish. As rivers swell with rain and overflow their banks, barbs travel into the growing, food-rich shallows of the floodplains. They profit from their natural ability to adjust to the opportunities a rapidly shifting ecosystem has to offer. The floods are the breeding period for many fish, and barbs are no exception. As the waters recede, many adventurous barbs get trapped in seasonal pools, cut off from the river's flow. In bodies of water that don't dry up, many will survive in the slow-moving, often polluted, and oxygen-poor ponds until the next rains. While we may hate to admit it, many aquariums are not unlike nature's dry season barb traps.

Our treatment of *Barbus* is far from complete, as the enormous number of species in the group obliges us to pick and choose. Many behaviorally interesting barbs are silvery and colorless, and therefore rarely sold. Others are just a bit too large for the commercial importers, who generally find fish over 3 inches (7.6 cm) difficult to sell. Many barbs have enough going for them to be imported occasionally, and we will glance at those species, but other interesting species have no real presence outside the tanks of specialists in the group.

Barbus tetrazona—The Tiger Barb
Bleeker 1855
Indonesia, Sumatra, Borneo
3 inches (7.6 cm)

In the aquarium hobby, the tiger barb may be the most popular member of the group. It has lovely, bright colors and a striking patterning to go with its always active behavior, even under the stressful conditions offered in the pet shop.

Unlike the case of many aquarium fish, there is no need to guess what a tiger barb will develop into when you get them home; they are only too happy to show off their finery, no matter what. All that aside, they may be the worst ambassadors for the group. Tiger barbs have shredded more fins and killed more tankmates than probably any other fish their size. They have given the barb family a pretty bad reputation in the hobby. Their great popularity has been a brake on the popularity of their family.

Tiger barbs are great to keep in either single-species tanks, or in mixed *Barbus* tanks. They are fish with a need for hierarchy, and a constant need to work out their rank within their mobile schools. When they encounter other fish, they treat them as they would other tetrazona. A fish that doesn't show an appropriate (in tiger barb terms) response will be endlessly bullied. If kept in groups of six or more, this aggression may be kept within the family, but even then, belligerent individuals can annoy or injure docile tankmates.

If an aquarist opts for this attractive fish, a large tank is in order. Also, they will need tough companions that will rapidly communicate their unwillingness to play to these curious and nippy barbs. Central American cichlids are geographically unlikely tankmates, but they get along famously with tiger barbs.

These fish are commercially bred in huge numbers, and are not hard to breed at home. A pair should be kept in a planted, warm (80°F [27°C]) tank with lots of fine-leaved plants. The eggs take about a day and a half to hatch. Males are thinner, smaller, and slightly more brightly colored than females.

There are a number of artificially selected versions of this fish, including an interesting-looking moss green morph, and an albino form. At times, the original tiger form of the fish can be harder to find than the novelty aquarium strains.

Barbus conchonius—The Rosy Barb
Hamilton 1822
Northern India
6 inches (15 cm), although usually half this size in aquaria

The rosy barb is as active as the tiger barb, but these colorful clowns are more inclined to put their energy into eating than fighting. Generally, they stay at around 3 inches (7.6 cm), and males, while slimmer and longer than females, have a lovely rose pink to red glow in spawning season. Since well-fed individuals of this forgiving species will spawn almost daily, drabness is not an issue with these fish.

Hobby lore says this fish spawns only in shallow water; however, the authors have observed breeding activity in deep tanks, if there is a space between plants and the water surface. They are best spawned above grates or marbles. Rosys, which will eat anything remotely resembling food, are voracious egg eaters.

Their tank should be tailored to their size and high level of activity. They don't generally bother other fish, although their frenetic playfulness can stress placid tankmates. They get along very well with cichlids and other traditionally rough company. They like cooler tanks (65° to 75°F [18°–24°C]).

Barbus arulius
Jerson 1849
Southern India
4.25 inches (11 cm)

Once an aquarist is hooked on barb keeping, this becomes a must-have species. Unfortunately, it is only occasionally available, in spite of its superb dorsal fin and delicate colors. Males have dark red to blackish extensions on their dorsals, over a barred body that, while basically light brown and silver, has shades of red, green, and blue, depending on the lighting. The catch with this heavy-bodied fish is that the lovely coloration develops only on mature specimens, which are much too large for the tastes of most aquarists. It really is a species for a barbs-only community tank of mid-sized species.

Barbus cumingii—Cumming's Barb
Guenther 1868
Sri Lanka
2 inches (5 cm)

Cumming's barbs are not often seen in most pet shops, but are not especially rare either. Their energy and hardiness have kept them in the hobby, even if their colors are not especially striking. These lively, peaceful barbs are worth waiting for, as they are good community fish, especially when they can move between light and shade. As is usual with barbs, the male is lighter-bodied, and males of *cumingii* have more colorful tail (caudal) fins. They need clean water.

Barbus denisonii—The Red Flash Shark
Day 1865
India
6 inches (15 cm)

This barb is one of the most beautiful fish in the family. The crimson red streak on the front of its body is one of the most intense colors seen on any aquarium fish. Unfortunately this is a very sensitive species that does not transport well, and high losses are common when this species is shipped from its native India. In the aquarium, the red flash shark is a nervous schooling fish

Tiger Barbs (Barbus tetrazona) *are seen in every pet store around the world.*

The green or moss Tiger Barb is an aquarium form.

The white Tiger Barb.

that does well in planted larger tanks. A second form, or maybe species, with a smaller, higher body, a bright red dorsal, and more red on its flanks is sometimes imported as *denisonii.*

Barbus everetti—The Clown Barb
Boulenger 1894
Southeast Asia
4 inches (10 cm)

As aquarium fish, clown barbs are in the same class as *Barbus arulius.* They are attractive, peaceful warm-water barbs that few seem to keep, as they are rarely seen. Males are brighter-colored and lighter-bodied than females. The fish are overall golden yellow, with broken green-black bars on their flanks. The fins can be pale red. They are plant spawners that need a lot of room to move, and should be kept and bred in large tanks. Clown barbs are sensitive to oodinium, and are noteworthy jumpers.

Barbus eugrammus
Silas 1956
Malaysia
4.25 inches (11 cm)

This quiet, timid barb features a series of stripes running horizontally from its head to its caudal fin. It is attractive, but its shyness and size have kept it out of the mainstream hobby. While it behaves like a much smaller fish, it is a touch too big for the average community tank. It is easy to breed and raise, but difficult to find.

Barbus fasciatus—The Banded Barb
Jerdon 1849
Southeast Asia
5.5 inches (14 cm)

Fasciatus is an uncommon visitor to our fish tanks, but an interesting one when it can be

The longfin variety of the Rosy Barb.

The large but delicate Barbus denisonii *is a beautiful addition to a well-planted aquarium.*

found. It likes to be kept in the mid-70s°F (mid-20s°C), and needs a school or it will do poorly. This is an active species once it gets over its shyness. Once they have matured, adults are crimson red beauties that are a must-have for most barb enthusiasts.

Barbus filamentosus
Valenciennes 1842
India, Sri Lanka
5.5 inches (14 cm)

This is a pretty and active mid-sized barb that likes room to swim. It is hardy, tolerant,

The Clown Barb (**Barbus everetti**) *can be difficult to find in aquarium shops.*

Only mature red Banded Barbs (**Barbus fasciatus**) *develop full color.*

The Golden Dwarf Barb (**Barbus gelius**) *should be seen much more often than it is.*

and not especially demanding, except when it comes to the size of its aquarium.

Barbus gelius—The Golden Dwarf Barb
Hamilton 1822
Central India
1.5 inches (3.8 cm)

This tiny, perky barb can look more like a rasbora than a *Barbus*. Its size and activity level make it ideal for a community of small fish. *Barbus gelius* is not colorful, as, depending on the light, it will be either transparent or vaguely golden, with irregular flank blotches and a red (on males) caudal to head stripe. Females are heavier-bodied. In spite of the delicacy of its coloration, this is a fish worth keeping for its behavior. It is also a candidate for an unheated tank, as *Barbus gelius* like to be kept from the mid-60s°F to low 70s°F (18-22°C). They are not difficult to coax into breeding, in a tank planted with cryptocorynes.

Barbus lateristrigata—T-Barb, Spanner Barb
Valenciennes 1842
Southeast Asia
7 inches (18 cm)

Small specimens of this attractive barb have been common in pet shops since the post-World War I era. However, not many aquarists realize the growth potential of the T-Barb, although it rarely approaches its maximum size in captivity. It is a nonaggressive species, that needs hiding places and tends to become more solitary as it ages. It comes in a number of color varieties, as its range is immense. Males tend to be more colorful than females of this easy-to-breed, warm water fish. If you start with healthy stock and maintain good water quality, these fish are almost indestructible.

Barbus narayani
Hora 1937
Sri Lanka
3 inches (7.6 cm)

This is an example of a peaceful, rather shy, and rare barb, the kind of fish that destroys the aquarium hobby stereotype of barbs as common, well-known creatures. It is an attractive and interesting species that has yet to be imported in the numbers that would allow it to catch on.

Barbus nigrofasciatus—The Black Ruby Barb
Guenther 1868
Sri Lanka
2.5 inches (6.35 cm)

The black ruby barb was once a more popular fish, but it never should have lost its following. It is an active, peaceful, and somewhat shy species that gets along with most similarly marked barbs, and fits into mixed communities quite well. The larger males are more colorful, and the fish can be bred with a grate or plants in a tank at the high 70s°F (mid- to high 20s°C). It is easy to feed, but likes flake with a vegetable content. Always keep an eye out for ich and oodinium with these fish.

Barbus oligolepis—The Checkered Barb
Bleeker 1853
Indonesia, Sumatra
5.5 inches (14 cm), usually smaller

This quick-growing, easy-to-find barb is especially pretty when it is small. Males are larger with black-edged fins. They spar among themselves, rarely doing any damage with these ritualized and attractive displays. They are a good community fish in schools, and breed in pairs near the surface under the same conditions as black ruby barbs. They like cool water, but it must be clean or they are prone to ich.

Barbus pentazona pentazona— The Five-banded Barb
Boulenger 1894
Southeast Asia, Singapore, Malaya, Borneo
2 inches (5 cm)

This more slender *Barbus* is not common, and has on occasion been confused with *B. tetrazona,* the tiger barb. It is a peaceful schooling species that is limited in the hobby by the difficulty of breeding it. There are a number of geographic color variants or sub-species of this barb.

A similar tiger barb is *Barbus partipentazona* from Thailand. It is easier to breed than *penta-zona,* but shows levels of rowdiness compara-ble to *Barbus tetrazona.*

Barbus phutunio
Hamilton 1822
India, Sri Lanka
2 inches (5 cm)

This is a rare fish but one that has its charm. It is a very high-bodied, yet tiny barb. Its timid nature makes it a small specimen for mid-sized or larger tanks, as it should be kept in groups. Individual fish tend to stay alone, sparring harmlessly with other *phutunio* when their paths cross. It likes a cool period in winter, and is extremely delicate.

Barbus rhomboocellatus—The Rhomboid Barb
Koumans 1940
Borneo
2 inches (5 cm)

This barb illustrates part of the attraction of its group. It is a mysterious, extremely pretty fish that is rarely imported. It may not have been spawned in captivity. In spite of its robust body shape, it is a shy, delicate blackwater fish. Once it has accli-mated to captivity, it can adapt to moderately hard water, but if the water quality deteriorates, it is very susceptible to oodinium and ich.

What makes it a desirable aquarium fish is its color. It has the reddish orange shades we expect on a tiger, set off by interesting, rhom-boid, vertical bars. It stays in the shadowed parts of the tank, and is very striking as it moves in its school through plants. Hopefully, it will become more available in the near future.

Barbus schwanenfeldii—The Tinfoil Barb
Bleeker 1853
Southeast Asia
13 inches (35 cm)

It seems that every generation of aquarium keepers has a fish it wants to try keeping in spite of everyone knowing it will outgrow its home. The tinfoil barb had its turn during the 1960s and 1970s, and effectively outgrew its welcome in the mainstream hobby. Juveniles were once staples of the trade, but fewer of these heavy-bodied beauties are crammed into inadequately sized tanks these days. Unfortu-nately, many Asian fish farms reacted to the drop in popularity of the fish by deciding to change it. Some specimens are injected with red or blue dyes, which, while possibly harming the fish, also fade very rapidly—within three to four months. An albino form has also been introduced. None of these marketing strategies address the fundamental difficulty of the size of this fish. The beauty of the natural form has never been a problem. For those with very large, well-lit tanks, these highly reflective, hardy fish earn the comparison to tinfoil.

The T-Barb (Barbus lateristrigata) *is a hardy species, larger than most barbs seen in the aquarium hobby.*

The Rhomboid Barb (Barbus rhombooccellatus) *is most comfortable in soft, acidic water.*

Barbus narayani *is native to Sri Lanka.*

The large, yet popular Tinfoil Barb (Barbus schwanenfeldii).

The Checkered Barb (Barbus oligolepis) *is a small species, well-suited for the community tank.*

The gold or "schuberti" form of **Barbus semifasciolatus.**

Barbus semifasciolatus—Schubert's Barb, The Golden Barb
Guenther 1868
Southeast China
4 inches (10 cm)

All scientific descriptions of fish have to give information on where the fish originates. In the past, some hobbyists described fish from commercial importations, and the results were confusing at best (also see *Danio "frankei"*). The golden barb has very little hobby presence as itself, but as *Barbus schuberti* has appeared in many tanks and books. While the origins of Schubert's barb are a mystery, it was likely a color form bred in the United States and exported with a pseudoscientific name that caught on.

Like many Chinese fish, it tolerates subtropical temperatures (64°–75°F [18°–24°C]), is hardy, easy to breed, and eats anything. These fish are very prolific, golden yellow barbs that can be sexed by the usual body-weight method.

Barbus ticto—The Ruby Barb, The Odessa Barb
Hamilton 1822
India, Sri Lanka
4 inches (10 cm)

Barbus stoliczkanus
Day 1871
Eastern Myanmar
3 inches (7.6 cm)

Both of these *Barbus* are old-timers in the hobby, and *stoliczkanus* is generally treated as a subspecies of *ticto*. They are lively barbs that are easy to keep and breed. Their active natures mean they must be kept in schools of at least six. The form of *stoliczkanus* that comes in as a wild import is quite different in coloration

The Odessa Barb (Barbus ticto) *is an ideal aquarium fish.*

Barbus stoliczkanus, *a subspecies of the Odessa Barb.*

from the standard *tictos*. Its main distinguishing feature is its jaunty red dorsal fin, which is edged in black on males.

Barbus ticto is mainly famous for a selected form, the Odessa barb, which had its origins in the Russian aquarium hobby. The accompanying photo is of a spectacular wild form. It is kept much like the rosy barb.

Barbus titteya—The Cherry Barb
Deraniyagala 1929
Sri Lanka
2 inches (5 cm)

While an aquarist might say the cherry barb is very common, an ecologist would consider

Barbus titteya to be a great rarity. Cherry barbs are an endangered species in the wild, and only the great ease with which they can be commercially bred allows us to see and keep them. It would be tragic if this fish were to disappear from its habitat and take on an existence solely in the artificial world of the aquarium hobby, but that may be its fate. Early overfishing for the hobby, combined with habitat degradation from an ever-expanding human population, have not allowed this prolific animal to bounce back in the shrinking number of slow-moving, vegetated pools that produce it.

Cherry barbs are an anomaly when it comes to shape, with their slender, low-backed profile. Males in their bright cherry spawning garb are striking fish. They are not hard to breed in slightly acid water in the mid-70s°F (mid-20s°C). The fish can be kept in groups, but will often spread out within the tank, living relatively solitary lives in comparison to other barbs.

In the hobby, they rival the tiger barb in availability, a testament to how easy it is to raise their young. There is an albino strain available, but it does not share the hardiness of the unselected form.

Barbus vittatus
Day 1865
India, Sri Lanka
2.25 inches (5.7 cm)

Barbus vittatus is a hardy, calm fish that demands little, and shows up occasionally. It usually looks rather dull and silvery in the pet store, but once acclimated to a clean and planted aquarium, it is a very attractive fish.

African Barbus

African barbs are nowhere near as diverse as Asian species, largely due to some different elements in the ecosystem that produced them. While barbs are a dominant small-fish group in Asia, in Africa the competition is more complex. Asian barbs share their weedy streams and river floodplains with some very popular Anabantoids (labyrinth fish or gouramies) or, in coastal habitats, with a few killifish species. Their African cousins have to share the plants along the banks with Microctenopoma Anabantoids, killifish, dwarf cichlids, and most important, characins (African tetras). The latter group fills a very similar ecological role to barbs. This evolutionary logjam seems to have kept all African river fish groups under check—with the exception of the magnificently beautiful killifish genera. There aren't too many aquarium-appropriate barbs, small jungle cichlids, or tetras from Africa; as if to compensate, the species we do have can be very attractive.

Barbus jae
Boulenger 1903
Cameroon, Gabon
1.75 inches (4.5 cm)

Barbus jae is legendary in aquarium circles. It is one of the Holy Grails of those who specialize in small, delicate, hard-to-keep beauties. In a way, its reputation as difficult may be more due to the problems of shipping it than to what it does in the fish tank. While not prolific, it can be bred (males have brighter colors). The key seems to be getting it to settle in in the crucial week or two after it arrives. A single-species tank from the high 60s° to low 70s°F (19°–23°C), with soft water, and lots of plants and shade will give you a chance of success with these expensive, much sought-after barbs. The intensity of the firewagon red on some importations has to be seen to be believed.

Barbus fasciolatus—The Angola Barb
Gunther 1868
Angola, Zimbabwe, Zambia, Katanga
2 inches (5 cm)

This barb would be popular if it were available in the trade; however, importations have been sporadic at best, and breeding has not been done on a large scale. Often, it travels under the name *Barbus barilioides,* as it appears to have been scientifically described twice. The *barilioides* name has almost become a popular name for the fish. These barbs are similar in looks to *Barbus jae,* but lack the latter's complex coloration. Despite their size, they need a fair-sized aquarium, due to their active lifestyle. It can be hoped this reddish brown to red-violet, tiger-striped, and slender-bodied barb will become more available in the near future.

Barbus holotaenia
Boulenger 1904
Cameroon through to Angola
5 inches (13 cm)

Barbus holotaenia is an example of what can go wrong (and right) in purchasing obscure African barbs. This fish will often make an appearance as small, jaunty looking juveniles in shipments of other African fish. It is rarely imported on its own, but as what the trade calls a "mixer" or "contaminant," it will find its way into pet shops. The perky, pretty, active no-name barb you put in your community will grow at a prodigious rate, becoming an attractive, cigar-shaped silvery fish. Adult coloration for this peaceful, large barb consists of a simple

black line from the snout to the tail, over large silvery scales. It is a good option for a community of larger barbs in a large planted tank.

Barbus hulstaerti
Poll 1945
Gabon, Congo River region
1.5 inches (3.8 cm)

This retiring little barb needs to be kept in a small school, in a tank with stable water conditions and cover. It is a small bluish fish with a lovely yellow and black dorsal, and bright yellow anal and ventral fins. The body features attractive, strongly defined black blotches. It is a rarely seen species—the fact that it comes from the region affected by both constant warfare and the deadly Ebola virus has discouraged collectors—but one that any keeper of small species would love to see.

Barbus callipterus—The Cutter Barb
Boulenger 1907
West Africa (very widespread)
6 inches (15 cm)

Like *Barbus hulstaerti,* the cutter barb likes cooler water tropical tanks (around 68°F [19°C]). We often expect jungle streams to be hot, but deep in the rain forest, little sunlight gets through the forest canopy to warm water, and many African fish habitats rarely get above 70°F (20°C). While this is a given for killifish keepers, barb, African tetra, and dwarf cichlid fanciers often overlook this essential information.

Cutter barbs are a rare case where the common name says almost as much as the scientific name. There are a number of similar silvery barb species found together in the wild, and exported as *Barbus callipterus.* While widespread in nature, they have now become

Barbus jae **is perhaps the most colorful of the African barbs.**

The Cutter Barb (*Barbus callipterus*) **is widespread in Africa but rare in aquariums.**

Humphead Barbs (*Barbus camptacanthus*) **are beautiful schooling fish for larger tanks.**

rare even in specialists' tanks. Their size works against them, as does their lack of color. In a school in a well-lit large aquarium with fast-flowing filtration, their silver scales and restless behavior make for a flashy show.

Barbus camptacanthus—The Humphead Barb
Bleeker 1863
Cameroon, Nigeria, Gabon
6 inches (15 cm), usually smaller

This pretty barb occasionally hitchhikes in on African shipments, although its adult size usually keeps it out of the hobby on its own merits. It is a peaceful schooling barb, with a reputation for eating the leaves of soft plants. For those familiar with the very successful North American cyprinid minnows of the dace group, this is yet another fascinating example of creatures far apart evolving a similar body plan. The superficial resemblance is striking, despite the African barb's large scales and different color pattern.

Danios

Our next group is the Asian danios. This group was long divided into danio and brachydanio; however, recent research seems to be leaning toward eliminating brachydanio as a genus. The main differences between the two groups would appear to have been based on size. One fish from this large group, the Zebra danio *(Danio rerio),* has enjoyed close to a century of popularity in aquaria, without losing ground to the many new introductions that have appeared since its debut in the very early days of the twentieth century. For many hobbyists, this is the first egg layer they set up to breed, and the sight of an easy-to-produce swarm of baby zebras has entertained aquarists since before World War I. The restless darting of the ever-active adults has also lost none of its appeal. Many aquarists use a school of danio-type barbs to stir things up in a community that has become too placid.

Danios are a growth industry in the modern hobby, as the old schema, in which half a dozen species were common to the point of boring experienced hobbyists, is giving way before the introduction of a number of desirable newly described or discovered species. These new introductions make danios as intriguing to modern fans of small fish as they were to our great-grandparents' generation.

One constant has been the techniques used for spawning danio species. These fish will spawn on plants, but most hobbyists favor the use of spawning grates or boiled marbles to hide the large quantities of eggs.

Danio rerio—The Zebra Danio
Hamilton 1822
Eastern India
2.25 inches (5.7 cm)

Zebra danios are ditch fish par excellence. In the wild, these torpedo-shaped barbs inhabit flowing, oxygenated streams and ditches, generally fringed with overhanging plants. These tiny fish rely on speed, camouflage, and the proximity of cover to survive. Any aquarist who has attempted to net zebras from a planted aquarium can attest to their skill in evading predators. If you ever keep a large group of these fish and startle them under a bright light, you will see how safety in numbers and unexpected coloration work together to confuse predators.

This is a very important fish, and not just for what we as hobbyists can observe. Zebras may

The Meteorite Danio (Danio shanensis) is among the interesting, recently arrived danios in the aquarium hobby.

The albino Zebra fish (Danio rerio).

The familiar Zebra fish is one of the most popular aquarium species ever known.

be one of the most seriously studied vertebrates out there. The scientific community loves them as research subjects, and the genetics of *Danio rerio* have already been extensively mapped out,

Ornaments Versus Armaments

✔ The small fish we keep in aquariums are incredible things, when we consider that in the wild, almost everything eats them; even humans catch tiny *Barbus pentazona* to make a popular bottled fish sauce.

✔ Evolution has supplied these creatures with many defensive weapons, including the confusing color patterns we find beautiful, abilities to survive in shallow water, and most important, the capacity for high-speed evasive maneuvers.

✔ The many breeder-produced long-finned barbs, danios, and minnows are good sellers, but the artificially selected finnage obscures any attempt to understand how these tiny fish evolved to survive in their complex, natural environments.

✔ The ornamental long-finned mutants are also at a great disadvantage if kept together with natural forms. They are slower to get to food, and do poorly in the pecking order of an active school.

✔ Long-finned rosy barbs, white mountain cloud minnows, zebras, or other fish probably should not be combined with their natural form brethren.

with much more work in progress. They are used in a wide range of research projects.

Adult fish are easy to sex, based on body bulk. Males are extremely slender in comparison to females. Hobbyist opinion is divided on their social structure, with some noting a loyalty among mated pairs, while others suggest that spawning is easy to trigger by adding slightly cooler, oxygenated water to a mid- to high 70s°F (23°–27°C) tank containing two to three males per female. Some like to spawn them in planted tanks, others in sterilized marble-bottomed setups. As previously noted, in single-species tanks, young can go grow up naturally with their parents' school. Zebras may be popular subjects for scientific research, but as we can see, they leave a lot of room for hobbyist experimentation too.

These readily available and inexpensive fish are also available in artificially selected albino and long-finned forms, although the long fins provide enough drag to take the elegance out of the fishes' swimming technique.

Danio albolineatus—The Pearl Danio
Blyth 1860
Myanmar, Thailand, Sumatra, Malaya
2.25 inches (5.7 cm)

As far as behavior and needs go, there is little difference between pearl and zebra danios. Like zebras, *albolineatus* swim restlessly, jump frequently, and spawn easily. Males are smaller and slightly more vibrantly colored than the larger, bulkier females. This fish is deceptively beautiful. In a pet store, under overly strong lighting or from a distance, it would seem to be very plain. Kept with a dark bottom or background, floating plants to provide some shade, and tanks long enough to allow it to behave naturally, the pearl danio takes on a violet, blue pearly shine that is unmatched in the aquarium hobby. It may be a fish only for hobbyists prepared to look closely at their fish, but once it has been seen in all its glory, it develops a permanent role in many community tanks.

Danio choprai—The Red Neon Danio, The Glowlight Danio
Hora 1928
Northern Myanmar
2 inches (5 cm)

This vivid tiny danio has recently gone from being just another name on the list of described danio species to being a creature with a great future in the hobby. Its colors guarantee it will be a much sought-after fish, once captive breeding programs have developed for it. Perhaps the easiest way to describe it is as a fish with the shape of a danio and the red-copper glow of one of the tiny rasbora. Once seen, it is hard to forget.

Danio "frankei"
Meincken 1963
2.5 inches (6.35 cm)

This spotted danio is now considered to be probably an aquarium-produced mutant, erroneously described as a naturally occurring species. Experts consider it most likely a mutant form of *Danio rerio,* although other sources are possible. This danio has quite a presence in older aquarium literature, but has only occasional availability in stores. Actually, *D. frankei* remains a bit of a mystery fish, incredibly common in the aquarium store tanks of some regions, and never seen in others.

Danio kerri
Smith 1931
Thailand
2 inches (5 cm)

This is a discrete little danio with a marginal place in the aquarium world. It comes in a variety of subtly different color forms.

Danio kyathit
Fang 1998
Myanmar
2 inches (5 cm)

At a first glance, this newly described danio might be mistaken for *Danio rerio.* If you find some and take them home, they will develop into a beautiful variation on an already popular plan. Males have *rerio*-like striping, but on the robust females, the belly stripes break up into "*frankei*-like" spot patterns. Both sexes feature bright red-orange fins, a feature that is easily radically intensified by the feeding of commercial color foods. Since this colorful fish breeds easily in the manner of *rerio,* the reign of the zebra as queen of the aquarium danios may face a serious challenge.

Danio nigrofasciatus—The Burmese Spotted Danio
Day 1869
Myanmar
2 inches (5 cm)

This pretty little danio is both quieter and more delicate than its close cousins. Spotted danios don't tear up and down the tank with the abandon of *rerio* or *albomarginatus.* They like slightly warmer water (high 70s°F [mid- to high 20s°C]) than *rerio. Nigrofaciatus* is a nice fish that for some reason has always been more popular in Europe than in North America.

Danio pathirana
Kottelat and Pethiyagoda 1990
Sri Lanka
2.5 inches (6.35 cm)

This robust, high-bodied danio has the sad distinction of being a critically endangered species. It is available to the hobby under interesting circumstances, as Sri Lankan collectors voluntarily suspended captures when the status of the fish became known, and instead concentrated on captive breeding of the fish.

This danio has an interesting ecology, as it tends to stay in one area of its pool or flowing stream habitat. It lives in small, surface-oriented schools of rarely more than six fish. Hopefully, we will not be the last generation fortunate enough to observe this attractive, peaceful species.

The Giant Danios

Giant danios are not the giants they seemed to be in the early days of the hobby, when large aquariums were extremely rare, but they do reach sizes of 4 to 6 inches (10 to 15 cm). They have lost a lot of popularity as Australasian rainbowfish have gained a following among keepers of larger schooling aquarium fish. There are two main species, with some occasional visitors in the group.

Danio aequipinnatus (McClelland 1839) is the well-known Giant Danio of the pet trade. It comes from India and Sri Lanka. Another similar fish, this time from Pakistan, northern India, and Bangladesh is *Danio devario* (Hamilton 1822). *Danio regina* (Fowler 1934), from southern Thailand, is rarer.

Danio-like Fish

There are a number of small groupings or single-species genera that are very similar to danios, and will appeal to people who enjoy keeping small, fast-moving minnows. As we work through this complex patchwork of species and genera, remember that this is a totally artificial grouping, thrown together for our convenience as hobbyists.

Chela dadyburjori
Menon 1952
Southeast Asia
1.75 inches (4.5 cm)

Chela dadyburjori are small fish with no consistent presence in the aquarium world. This is unfortunate, as they are intriguing little animals, attractive to anyone who already likes small danios. While they lack the restlessness of the latter, they are active, busy fish that stay in the top section of the tank, but not at the surface. Much like other small barbs, they need to be kept in groups; however, if numbers fall below six, they will join in the schools of other small Asian barbs. They do well in the company of slender rasbora species, and danios, especially *nigrofasciatus*. With their brassy color, deep blue-black lateral line, and porthole pattern on the side, these long-lived, hardy fish can provide a pleasing contrast to their flashier tankmates for many years.

Chela caeruleostigmata—The Asian Blue Hatchetfish
Smith 1931
Thailand
2.25 inches (5.7 cm)

This is an appealing, active-swimming community fish we also don't often see. It is totally unrelated to the South America hatchetfish (Gasteropelecidae) group, in spite of its having a fairly deep keel.

Chela laubuca—The Indian Glass Barb
Hamilton 1822
Southeast Asia
2.25 inches (5.7 cm)

Chela laubuca is a moderately drab fish with an attractive body shape. While we don't see such colorless fish often, it is a peaceful community tank resident for those who do get to keep it. Beware: It is a prodigious jumper.

Tanichthys albonubes—The White Mountain Cloud Minnow, The White Cloud Mountain Minnow, The White Cloud, The Poor Man's Neon, The Meteor Minnow

Lin Shu-Yen 1932
Southern China
1.5 inches (3.8 cm)

Few fish have had as many great common names as the one we will call the White Cloud. These tiny mountain minnows are temperature-tolerant (from 42°F [5°C] to 78°F [27°C]) and extremely easy to breed in plants, or with fry growing up alongside their parents. It doesn't hurt that this hardy little aquarium staple is very beautiful. Back in the days when the South American neon tetra (*Paracheirodon innesi*, Myers 1936) was still a puzzle to breeders, white clouds were sold as the "poor man's neon" due to their ease of reproduction, inexpensive price, and extremely vivid juvenile colors. At another point in its aquarium history, a selected, long-finned aquarium strain gained a large following as the "meteor minnow." Aquarists of the 1950s will still argue that today's long-finned white clouds are pale imitations of the apparently lost "meteor" strain.

White clouds accept a wide range of water qualities, but do best in planted tanks. Parents should be removed after spawning if you want large numbers of young, but if your goal is to set up a mock Chinese stream in your home, a small aquarium with thick plants, no heater, and a sponge filter, a few white clouds (no other species), and feedings with fine-particle food (so that both adults and fry get nourishment) will

result in an ongoing, self-replenishing community of lovely minnows. Every aquarist should try keeping such a setup at least once.

Esomus Species—The Flying Barbs

There are a number of flying barbs from all across Southeast Asia. None are extremely popular, and all are somewhat difficult to identify due to their similarity. The species *Esomus danricus*, for example, has appeared under several different species names, with added subpopulations. Identification of individual species is challenging. The distinguishing features of the *Esomus* group include their "super barbels." These fish sport handlebar mustaches worthy of the dandiest Victorian cavalry officer, with barbels extending for half the length of their bodies. They are all minnow-shaped.

The Striped Flying Barb (Esomus metallicus) *is yet another member of a hard-to-identify group.*

Due to the confusion in identifying them, they are hard to approach species by species. They are generally quiet, often solitary, or loosely schooling barbs with black and gold lines from the caudal to behind their eyes. They like planted tanks, and are prodigious jumpers when disturbed.

Any aquarist looking to break new ground can probably find a lot to learn in studying the flying barb group.

Sawbwa resplendens
Annandale 1918
Myanmar
1.75 inches (4.5 cm)

This small shimmering bluish minnow is a perfect lesson in the concept of evolutionary convergence, as well as a first-rate aquarium fish. Most hobbyists are familiar with South America's "rummy-nose tetras" (*Petitella georgiae, Hemigrammus bleheri,* and *rhodostomus*). While it's already remarkable that three South American blackwater species in two different genera should have evolved crimson red snouts, we find a totally unrelated Myanmar barb with the same very distinctive characteristic. However, beyond the fact that the four species are all small, silver-bodied, and red-nosed, the parallels end. *Sawbwa* are hardwater fish that lose their beautiful red snout in the soft water in which many hobbyists, fooled by the similarities with the Rio Negro tetras, try to keep them. They are delicate in soft water, but when kept in small schools in low to mid-70s°F (low 20s°C) planted tanks with moderately mineral-rich water, they are lively, hardy, luminous little fish. It is not hard to get them to spawn, but the fry are extremely small and hard to feed without good live microorganism cultures.

Microrasbora rubescens—Red Dwarf Rasbora
Annandale 1918
Myanmar
1.5 inches (3.8 cm)

It can be said the red dwarf rasbora is small, but it is rarely red in captivity. At best, it is generally a pinkish hardwater minnow, quite active and danio-like in its habits. In its natural habitat, this hardy creature is a popular baitfish. It should be kept and bred under the same conditions as *Danio erythromicron.*

Microrasbora erythromicron—The Emerald Dwarf Rasbora
Annandale 1918
Myanmar
1 inch (2.5 cm)

This little rasbora type may end up reclassified as a danio, although at the time of writing, the jury still seems to be out. For many aquarists, this genus change would take some getting used to. Under any name, it is a shy, ornately, yet discretely colored fish that needs a planted tank to draw it out into open water. It is a good community fish with equally small, peaceful species, but when kept with more robust fish, it will disappear into whatever cover the tank offers and rarely come out. Males of the species are more brightly colored and thinner than females. The emerald dwarf rasbora breeds easily in fine-leaved plants.

Rasboras

The fish most commonly kept in the hobby under the name of "the Rasbora" isn't even a rasbora anymore. Confused? The old tried-and-true genus of *Rasbora* is being revised, and the result is that there are a lot of new genus names for hobbyists to get used to. It would appear from even a superficial look at the group that the changes have just begun. This is a large group (though the number of aquarium species is limited) and contains a variety of related yet different-looking fish.

The reclassifications are interesting ones that add much to our understanding of the fish, but that does not mean that they won't raise eyebrows for awhile. In the interests of convenience, we will keep the section heading of "Rasbora" as we discuss fish that will appear under a series of new names. For those who are encountering the group for the first time, remember that we have lumped them together like this as they are the species generations of aquarists called *Rasboras*.

This is one of the larger groups within the barb world. Unfortunately, many intriguing *rasbora* species are rarely if ever seen. To begin, there is the familiar problem of Asian schooling fish being less available in the trade than South American tetras. Then, there is the size problem. Several of the truly beautiful rasbora group fish are too small for the average aquarium. Two inches (5 cm) seems to be the measure of a popular small fish, and many one-time rasboras are half that size. On the other hand, there is an entire group of larger fish, popular for their size, but above the usual size cut off line.

Habitat can work against these fish too. Many of them are creatures of blackwater—the tannin-stained, mineral-poor water of rain forests. This hasn't kept the harlequin rasbora (*Trigonostigma heteromorpha*) from becoming a hobby-wide favorite for many decades, to the point where Singapore has put its image on a stamp. However, it has kept importers from exploring many other blackwater species with a reputation for being delicate.

"Spot the Harlequin"

It helps to know where your *Trigonostigma* are from to have a clear identification, but few aquarists have the luxury of such information. A thumbnail "harlequin field guide" to your pet shop may be useful for those who like to know what they are keeping:

✔ *T. heteromorpha* has a large triangle, filling most of the posterior flank.

✔ *T. hengeli* has a smaller, more lambchop-shaped patch, usually framed with red lines.

✔ *T. espei* (the rarest) has a small triangle, often framed with silver.

The final wrinkle is that some rasboras are supremely delicate. The group offers us species to challenge and delight fishkeepers of all experience levels.

Trigonostigma

This is the new genus set up by Kottelat and Witte in 1999. It consists of a small (four species) popular little group of small high-bodied fish with triangular patches on their flanks. Three of these fish show up labeled simply as "rasbora" in many pet shops, although only one (*heteromorpha*) can be considered commonly available. They are perky little fish that glow when they are happy, which in clean water is most of the time.

Trigonostigma heteromorpha—The Harlequin Rasbora
Duncker 1904
Southeast Asia
1.75 inches (4.5 cm)

As far as the hobby goes, this is the flagship species of the *Trigonostigma* group, usually

Trigonostigma heteromorpha is the popular beauty often sold as "the Harlequin Rasbora."

The White Harlequin is an artificially selected form of the Harlequin (Trigonostigma hengeli).

Another example of the fish breeder's art, the Black Harlequin.

identified under the name of the "harlequin rasbora." Millions of these fish are produced and exported annually from the fish farms of Singapore. This is a peaceful schooling fish, ideal for a community of small fish. It is kept much like many small South American characins (tetras). While it is a blackwater fish, it can be kept but not successfully bred in harder water, provided that water is kept clean. For viable young, you need to approximate the rain forest swamp conditions the species comes from (pH under 6.0, peat-filtered, and as soft as possible).

In dirty water, the species becomes fragile. Like many fish in the rasbora group, they can develop stubborn cases of velvet (oodinium) that will not be cured by the standard medications unless accompanied by large-scale water changes and an overall increase in water quality.

Harlequins spawn under leaves, and will often attempt to reproduce in well-maintained community tanks. The courtship colors of the fish are nothing short of spectacular, as the thinner-bodied male joins the heavier female in swimming upside down to lay and fertilize the adhesive eggs. Unfortunately, the eggs need extremely soft water to develop properly.

There are albino harlequins available, as well as a breeder-selected black form.

Trigonostigma hengeli—Hengel's Rasbora, Harlequin Rasbora
Meinken 1956
Sumatra
1.5 inches (3.8 cm)

The *hengeli* rasbora has appeared as often as "the harlequin fish" as it has under its own name. The similarities between the three "lambchop" (named for their side markings) *Trigonostigma* is a source of endless misidentification. Hengel's rasbora is more rare than *heteromorpha*, although it comes from the same sort of blackwater swamp habitats.

Trigonostigma espei—The Harlequin Rasbora, Espei's Rasbora, The Glowlight Rasbora
Meinken 1967
Thailand
1.5 inches (3.8 cm)

This is yet another hard-to-identify fish. In all aspects, of keeping and appearance, it is very similar to the other *Trigonostigma*. Just to complicate life, the common name often applied to this fish (the glowlight rasbora) is about as helpful as calling it a "harlequin," as *Rasbora pauciperforata* is also sold as a glowlight. There is also a popular glowlight tetra in the aquarium trade.

Boraras

The next group of ex-rasboras is the tiny fish of the genus *Boraras*. A school of Boraras in a moderate-sized aquarium will make your tank look like an ocean, while allowing the fish a much fuller range of activity than a larger fish would have in the same tank. The catch, once again, is that these fish ship poorly. Also, many consumers expect small fish to be extremely cheap, a fact that can make Boraras unappealing to importers.

Boraras maculatus—Dwarf Rasbora, Pygmy Rasbora
Duncker 1904
Southeast Asia
1 inch (2.5 cm)

This diminutive fish is the most commonly imported of the Boraras. As befits its size, it is for a community tank either with fish of its

An artificially selected gold form of the Harlequin.

Trigonostigma espei, *the tiniest Harlequin.*

The Dwarf Rasbora (**Boraras maculatus**) *is a beautiful, if sporadically available, fish.*

own genus, or with other tiny fish. It gets along well with *Trigonostigma*, small African barbs, and small South American tetras. Fish like angels *(P. scalare)* will find your beautiful Boraras to be a convenient snack.

Probably the best setup for Boraras is a tank with a 24-inch (60-cm) base, a dark background, and both rooted and floating plants. A sponge filter is adequate, and ideally—though not necessarily—the water should be soft and acidic. *B. maculatus* is hardy in clean water, though it shares the *Trigonostigma* tendency toward velvet in polluted water. It is not a fish you should buy on the first day it arrives in the store, as the sensitive fish ship badly, and should be observed for signs of sickness after arrival. Once the first few critical days are done, the fish can live a long life.

This fish is about as difficult to breed as *Trigonostigma,* under the same conditions. Use a heavily planted tank, and observe the pair closely for spawning behavior. Once there are eggs, remove the parents immediately, as they do not produce many eggs, and they will eat what they produce. You will need microscopic food for the fry.

Boraras brigittae
Vogt 1978
Southern Borneo, Indonesia
1.25 inches (3.5 cm)

Boraras merah
Kottelat 1991
Western and Southern Borneo
.75 inches (2 cm)

Only *Boraras merah* could make *Boraras brigittae* look big. Both are lovely little red fish, rarely imported but fascinating to keep in a microtank. At an adult size of under 1 inch (2.5 cm), *merah* is an amazingly small aquarium fish. It does very well in moderately hard water.

Boraras uropthalmoides—The Least Rasbora
Kottelat 1991
Asia
1.5 inches (3.8 cm)

This striped, silvery, and small rasbora has a wide distribution in nature, but is not flashy enough to have caught on in the hobby. It is an occasional import.

Sundadanio axelrodi—Axelrod's Rasbora
Brittan 1976
Indonesia, Sumatra
1.25 inches (3.5 cm)

This ex-rasbora sits all alone in its genus, something almost poetic for a fish this distinctive. Axelrod's rasbora is a most desirable fish, as the colors of an acclimated school moving through a planted tank are unforgettable. The blue form (pictured) will pick up any sidelighting and throw it back with a highly reflective metallic shine that is hard to equal. Despite their small size, a school of *axelrodi* is extremely eye-catching. There are red, blue, and gold varieties of this softwater, boraraslike fish sporadically available in the trade.

Rasboras
We finally come to the rasboras called (for now) "Rasbora."

Rasbora vaterifloris—The Ceylon Fire Barb, The Singhalese Fire Barb, The Fire Barb, The Purple Long-finned Rasbora, The Orange-finned Barb
Deraniyagala 1930
Sri Lanka
1.75 inches (4.5 cm)

Rasbora vaterifloris is a fish the average hobbyist sees once every few years. It is a beautiful species. Fire barbs are deep-bodied like harlequins, but either red or purple with longer fins than their cousins. The limiting factor in their hobby distribution is their sensitivity to poor water conditions, a fact that limits exporters' ability to successfully ship them. If they arrive healthy, they are relatively tough rasboras that can live for at least three years in a community tank.

There are a number of local color varieties of *vaterifloris;* however, when the authors have combined unequal numbers of distinctly purple and red fire barbs from different importations, it took very little time for all the fish to take on the colors of the majority.

Breeding fire barbs is not easy, as is the case with harlequins; however, for aquarists who luck into a school of these uncommon imports, it is a worthwhile project. Unless you live in a very large center, you should never count on seeing this beautiful fish become a regular visitor.

Rasbora kalochroma—The Clown Rasbora
Bleeker 1850
Western Malaysia, Borneo, Sumatra
4 inches (10 cm)

At one point, the diminutive *Boraras maculatus* was rumored to be the juvenile form of this spectacular rasbora. The two fish are quite similar in appearance, although the clown rasbora is five times the size of its cousin. These are peaceful, not overly social fish that seem to claim small territories in the plants. Their sensitivity to pollution and shipping stress is legendary. This is the main reason they are rarely seen.

Rasbora trilineata—The Scissortail Rasbora, The Three-lined Rasbora
Steindachner 1870
Western Malaysia, Sumatra, Borneo

6 inches (15 cm)

From the tiny rasboras, we go directly into a large, popular species. It is not especially hard to breed, readily available, and quite hardy, though it lacks the rich coloration of the smaller species. One problem with it is that males and females can be hard to tell apart, as the body-weight method for spotting females does not apply here. The fish needs room to move, given its size, but is a placid, peaceful schooling rasbora.

While there are a number of such moderately large rasbora species, most are silvery, with the nose to tail dark line that *trilineata* sports, but not the jaunty caudal markings. None of these other species have a consistent presence in the hobby.

Rasbora dorsiocellata—The Green-eyed Rasbora, The High-spot Rasbora, The Eye-spot Rasbora
Duncker 1904
Malayan Peninsula, Sumatra
2 inches (5 cm)

It is fascinating to see how basic fish coloration themes pop up again and again in the evolution of fish. As we have noted, there are Asian barb types bearing a striking resemblance to totally unrelated South American tetras. *Rasbora dorsiocellata* has the distinction of resembling a killifish group, the lampeyes. While at a quick glance, *dorsiocellata* appears to be a dull silvery fish, more and more hobbyists seem to be catching on to its unexpected beauty. Under indirect lighting, the eyes of these tiny fish reflect back a glowing emerald green. In a planted tank with a dark (ideally black) background, a school of *dorsiocellata* will attract the eye from yards (or meters) away. These fish are hardy and moderately easy

The name of the beautiful "fairy red" may change from Rasbora to Rasboroides.

"Nias" is an as-yet undescribed Rasbora species. There is much to be learned about this group of interesting fishes.

Scissortails (Rasbora trilineata) are popular for larger tanks.

to breed in a planted softwater tank. They eat their eggs. Males are slimmer than females.

The Striped Rasboras

Rasbora borapetensis
Smith 1934

Rasbora pauciperforata—The Glowlight Rasbora, The Red-lined Rasbora
Weber and de Beaufort 1916

Rasbora sp.—The Blackline Rasbora, The Brilliant Rasbora, The Red-tailed Rasbora
(unidentified)
Southeast Asia
2 inches (5 cm)

The brilliant or red-tailed rasbora is so popular that it seems to take more than one species to fill orders for it. The taxonomically inclined can debate the true identity of this lovely fish, but what seems clear is that more than one species appears on Asian shippers' lists, and therefore in aquarium stores, under these common names. The same phenomenon is known for *Rasbora pauciperforata* (Weber and de Beaufort 1916), a much sought-after species that seems to have various hard-to-identify danios and horizontally lined rasboras occasionally shipped under its name. This can be disappointing to informed aquarists, who expect the drab, stressed pet shop fish they buy to blossom under home aquarium conditions, to no avail. Predictably, the beautiful species never seem to be mistakenly identified as their drab cousins.

The hobby brilliant rasbora is a very pretty green-lined, minnow-shaped fish with a bright red caudal spot. It holds its colors under store

The "Brilliant Rasbora" (**Rasbora borapetensis**) *known in the aquarium hobby can be of several different species.*

Both **Rasbora borapetensis** *and* **R. dusnensis** *are offered to hobbyists as "Brilliant Rasboras."*

conditions. While those colors are striking when it is young, this long-lived rasbora does tend to fade slightly as it ages. It is a placid, schooling fish, capable of running with the danios when young, but inclined to hover around the plants as it ages. It is easy to breed in heavily planted softwater tanks, comfortable in a wide range of water conditions, tolerant of temperatures from the very low to high 70s°F (21°-26°C) and easy to find in the aquarium-fish trade.

Rasbora pauciperforata is also true to its colors in the pet shop. Its distinguishing feature is a vivid fluorescent pink/red horizontal line along the length of its body. It is a thinner, sharper-nosed, and more active fish than the red-tailed rasbora. In many ways, it looks like a stretch ver-

sion of South America's extremely popular glowlight tetra *(Hemigrammus erythrozonus).*

As for the various black and copper horizontally lined rasbora types that come in under the popular names, they seem to stay small and are attractive creatures in their own right. They are pleasant to keep, and hobbyists so inclined can learn a lot while searching for help on the identities of these fish on Asian Fisheries Internet sites. One of the great things about danio and rasbora keeping is that unlike other types of fish (catfish, cichlids, or even *Barbus*) the little mystery fish you bring home on a whim or by mistake is not going to grow up to eat the entire contents of your aquarium.

Loaches

The family of the loaches (Cobitidae) are carp-like fish that are closely related to the barbs and are ideal bottom dwellers for the community barb aquarium. They are popular in the general hobby, and have their own devoted core of specialists. A complicating factor in presenting them is the wide variety of species that are occasionally imported, and that then disappear from the hobby for years. Also, many

The Clown Loach (**Botia macracantha**) *may grow larger than many aquarists expect.*

loaches can become aggressive with age and tyrannize the aquarium. The attractive tiger loaches *(B. helodes, B. beauforti, B. hymeno-physa)* and redfin loaches *(B. modesta, B. rubripinnis)* are known for this.

We will concentrate on the most commonly available, peaceful species of this almost impossible-to-breed group.

Botia macracantha—The Clown Loach
Bleeker 1852
Indonesia, Sumatra, Borneo
12 inches (30 cm), usually half that size in captivity

Few fish are as easily recognizable as the clown loach. To this day all clown loaches in the trade are wild caught in Indonesia. There have been sporadic reports of them breeding in aquariums, but so far it seems that if this has happened, it has not been the result of anything but pure chance or hormone manipulation. Despite their large size (over 12 inches [30 cm] in the wild, rarely more than 6 inches [15 cm] in the aquarium), they are peaceful aquarium fish that make a striking addition to the community barb aquarium. Clown loaches should always be kept in groups and must be fed carefully, or they will waste away quickly. Too many aquarists wrongly assume bottom-oriented fish to be simply scavengers, capable of living on the leftovers of open-water fish.

The *Botia* species have a weapon (predictably, a barb) under their eye that can inflict painful cuts on careless keepers who handle the fish without being wary. They also use this built-in switchblade to defend against other fish. These loaches, like most naked (nonscaled) fish are extremely ich-sensitive, especially if kept too cool (below 82°F [28°C]). Clown loaches are avid and effective snail eaters. Some adults can be hard on plants, as they can have an odd habit of cutting stems at the bottom.

Botia morleti—The Skunk Loach
Tirant 1885
Northern India, Thailand
4 inches (10 cm)

Botia lohachata—The Striped Loach
Chaudhuri 1912
Northern India, Bangladesh
2.75 inches (7 cm)

These little loaches are hardy community species. They are much less aggressive among themselves than most *Botia* species and slightly hardier. In the beginning they are shy fish that will tunnel under rocks and driftwood, coming out only to eat. They will gain confidence as they slowly get used to the aquarium. They are relentless eaters of snails, a fact that adds to their popularity for many, but should be factored in before purchase.

Pangio kuhlii—The Kuhli Loach
Valenciennes 1846
Southeast Asia
4 inches (10 cm)

Despite being nocturnal, the kuhli loach has long been a favorite for community aquariums. These hardy and harmless fish hide in the roots of plants or bury themselves in the sand or under decorations during the day, and may not be seen for months at a time. Yet their active clownlike behavior when they do come out during the day, and their ability to scavenge leftover food from the smallest spaces in the aquarium at night, makes them useful community fish. Once caught by the thousands and shipped from Southeast Asia, kuhli loaches are becoming scarcer and are more difficult to find in stores. They have been bred in captivity. They lay bright green eggs in the roots of floating plants.

Stonesuckers

While they are sometimes marketed as loaches, the stonesuckers are a separate group (family Balitoridae). Due to their habits, and small size, they should become increasingly available in years to come.

Gastromyzon fasciatus—The Zebra Stonesucker
Sauvage 1878
Southern China
3.25 inches (8 cm)

Pseudogastromyzon myersi—The Green Stonesucker
Herre 1932
Borneo, Indonesia
2 inches (5 cm)

Stonesuckers are uniquely adapted to life in fast-flowing mountain streams. The fish is built to hang on in a strong current. In stagnant or old water it tends to get sick easily and die of bacterial infections; therefore, it needs frequent water changes and moderately cool oxygenated water. Little is known about its reproductive biology. This interesting group gives us ideal aquarium fish. Like the famous cichlids of Africa's Lake Malawi, stonesuckers eat *aufwuchs* (algae with insect larvae in it). In the aquarium, they require lots of plant-based food, and relish bloodworms.

Algae Eaters

Like most people, aquarists want miracles. One of the dreams of generations of fishkeepers has been to find a fish that devours all sorts of algae, and therefore keeps the tank clean and attractive with little human intervention. In the world of barblike fish, such an animal does exist. That's the good news. The bad news is more than one fish is sold as an "algae eater."

Gyrinocheilus aymonieri—The Chinese Algae Eater
Tirant 1883
Northern India, Thailand
11 inches (28 cm)

One of the tests to see if you are talking to an experienced aquarist is to ask about this fish. If the response you get is one of hostility toward the species, then you know you are talking to someone who has kept it. This member of the family Gyrinocheilidae is perhaps the most undeservedly popular aquarium fish in the hobby. While juveniles are hardy and nearly indestructible, fast-growing Chinese algae eaters become adults that have little interest in algae, but a pronounced taste for aquarium plants and for the protective slime coating on the flanks of their tankmates.

This nonalgae-eating fish has somehow become the algae eater in the trade, largely through its popular name. Southeast Asia offers many other species that are much better suited for this task, but they take a little more looking to locate. Siamese algae eaters are infinitely better at the job, so the Chinese algae eater should not find its way into a tropical community tank.

In its defense, *G. aymonieri* does tolerate cooler temperatures, and juveniles, below the

The Zebra Stonesucker (Gastromyzon fasciatus).

This is the albino phase of the Chinese Algae Eater.

Stonesuckers such as **Pseudogastromyzon myersi** *are becoming popular aquarium fish.*

The Flying Fox (Crossocheilus siamensis) *is a legendary algae eater.*

age when they lose interest in this diet may be good algae eaters with temperate water species in very large tanks.

Crossocheilus siamensis—The Siamese Algae Eater, The Siamese Flying Fox
Smith 1931
Thailand, Malaya
5.5 inches (14 cm)

This drab little fish is a much sought-after aquarium fish for planted tanks, as it does eat algae. It needs good filtration and room. Adults are territorial and do fight, but among themselves. This is one of the best algae-eating fish in the

The Chinese Algae Eater (Gyrinocheilus aymonieri) *becomes aggressive as it matures.*

*The shy Bala or Tricolor Shark (**Balantiocheilus melanopterus**) requires a large aquarium.*

*The Rainbow Shark (**Epalzeorhynchos erythrurus**) is far less aggressive than the Redtail Shark.*

*The Redtail Shark (**Epalzeorhynchos bicolor**) is a popular species for the aquarium.*

An albino Rainbow Shark.

hobby. In spite of its grouchiness toward its own species, it is most efficient when kept in schools.

Epalzeorhynchos kallopterus—The Flying Fox
Bleeker 1850
Northern India, Indonesia, Thailand, Sumatra, Borneo
6 inches (15 cm)

Because of its wide geographic range, this moderately effective algae eater is more commonly imported than the more efficient "Siamese" fish. Both fish are similar, with slender bodies, slightly higher backs, black stripes from the eye to the tail over olive bodies, and very

*The Marbled Shark (**Epalzeorhynchos variegatus**) is native to the Congo.*

erect dorsals. This species has two sets of barbels on its upper lip and dark markings on the dorsal, which is clear for the single-barbeled Siamese algae eater. We will see more fish from this genus under the category of "Sharks."

The Giant Barbs and "Sharks"

There are a lot of fish that are very cute when they are small, but if we don't inform ourselves about what they will become as they age, we can be in for some nasty surprises. A fish too big for your tank can be hard to get rid of. Shops don't want these unsalable behemoths, and few of us appreciate the ethics behind killing a pet because it has become inconvenient. Large fish from any group tax our resources by requiring not only larger tanks but also powerful filtration and far greater attention to water quality.

The problem begins in the pet shop, as many employees of lower-quality shops do not always realize what they are selling. Many stores will readily sell giant tinfoil barbs, tricolor sharks, and hifin sharks, and few shoppers take the necessary time to research their community tank fish in advance. When you encounter a pretty little fish you have never seen before, you should never buy it unless you can find information on its captive needs, size, and adaptability. All good stores will offer access to books like this to any hobbyist who asks.

The giant barbs demand ample room to grow. Aquariums to hold groups of giant barbs should be as close to 6 feet long (2 m) as possible. Nearly all of the giants eat or destroy plants and smaller tankmates, and tend to rearrange the decoration in an inappropriately setup aquarium. If you have a large tank equipped for big fish, with no small fish in it, they can be a lot of fun. Many fishkeepers develop much more of a pet-owner relationship with these fish, as psychologically, many people are more comfortable with bigger creatures. Most large aquarium Cypriniformes are perfect fish to complement popular cichlid species, or in tanks on their own. A tank of adult-sized tinfoil barbs in direct sunlight is one no fishkeeper will ever forget.

You will have noticed the word "sharks" in the heading for this section. The aquarium industry long ago recognized the marketability of the label "shark" to sell fish, even if they have only little resemblance to the actual ocean predator. Many of our common aquarium barbs are sold under this label. Most are peaceful, but can require larger tanks and more room than the common aquarium barbs.

The Redtail and Rainbow Sharks

Balantiocheilus melanopterus—The Bala, Silver, or Tricolor Shark
Bleeker 1851
Malaysia, Borneo, Thailand, Sumatra
24 inches (60 cm)

Few large fish have been more successful at becoming unlikely staples in the community tank than this one. The Bala shark is a very skittish, nervous fish that requires a tank of at least 4 feet (122 cm) in length to develop properly. For its size, the fish is extremely peaceful and can be kept with most smaller fish (within reason). Males are more slender and slight of body than females, but the Bala shark has never been bred in the confines of the home aquarium. In Thailand these fish are bred for the aquarium industry in outdoor mud ponds, where they readily produce thousands of young.

Epalzeorhynchos bicolor—The Redtail Shark
Smith 1931
Thailand
6 inches (15 cm)

Epalzeorhynchos erythrurus—The Rainbow Shark
Fowler 1937
Northern Thailand
5 inches (13 cm)

With their eye-catching coloration and sharklike forms, these are popular aquarium fish. *Epalzeorhynchos* are active fish that spend much time in the front of the aquarium and can entertain their keepers by swimming upside down and sideways. They are territorial and prefer to have a cave or other hiding place to retreat to. Juveniles of both species eat some algae but do not harm plants. Problems arise when the fish reach maturity. They have justifiably earned a reputation for age-related grouchiness. Redtail sharks are especially inclined to get nasty with members of their own species, and are more than ready to extend their aggression to any other fish in their tank.

Nearly all of the usually very young specimens available in pet stores are bred in Thailand through the use of hormone injections.

There is also a very attractive albino form of the rainbow shark available in the trade.

Labeo chrysophekadion—The Black Shark
Bleeker 1849
30 inches (75 cm)

This very large shark is sometimes offered in stores. Its maximum size is close to 30 inches (76 cm). Black sharks are among the most aggressive aquarium fish, ready and willing to kill much larger and stronger tankmates with constant and well-aimed attacks. Although young black sharks are sometimes sold by pet stores, this species should never be kept in a community tank.

Labeo variegatus—The Marbled Shark
Pellegrin 1926
Congo River System
14 inches (35 cm)

The mottled shark from the Congo River is a very beautiful fish when young, though it is not often seen in stores. As is the case with its Asian cousins, adults may become aggressive and have to be removed from the aquarium. These fish are fast swimmers that can be kept as dither or target fish with large cichlids, catfish, and even African puffers.

Myxocyprinus asiaticus—The Chinese Hifin Shark
Weber and de Beaufort 1916
Northern China
24 inches (60 cm)

Juveniles of this popular Chinese food fish are truly striking and bear a great resemblance to the marine batfish. In recent years, this brought them onto the aquarium market in large numbers. Unfortunately, their subtle beauty fades with age, as the fish get down to the serious business of growing. Adults are brown or gray; they attain lengths of over 2 feet (61 cm) and lose their juvenile shape with its high extension on the dorsal fin.

When hifin sharks first became available to hobbyists, the price for young specimens was very high; however, as their reputation has

Juvenile Hifin Sharks (**Myxocyprinus asiaticus**) *grow into large, drab adults.*

Probarbus julienni *is a popular food fish in Thailand but is listed as an endangered species.*

The Crossbanded Barb (**Puntioplites bulu**).

spread, the fish have fortunately begun to lose popularity and their prices declined.

Luciosoma trinema—The Apollo Shark
Bleeker 1855
Southeast Asia
23 inches (60 cm)

The body shape of the pike has a way of showing up in many fish families. This large, active, schooling "pike" is the barb entry into the game. It has a certain popularity in North America, but keeping schooling fish this size means they are often kept in what are for them difficult conditions. If you do have a huge aquarium and want to try *trinema*, make sure you have a good tank cover. Fish of close to 2 feet (61 cm) that like leaping have a way of making their presence felt in your house.

Conclusion

At a first glance, a hobbyist may think of barbs as being the few *Barbus* species we see in the neighborhood pet store; however, once we dig a little deeper, we see that barbs are diversity itself. Our quick study of the aquarium Cypriniformes has allowed us little more than a quick peek into the nature of barbs. This one grouping has evolved remarkable body forms and colors, but it has also developed remarkable survival strategies and behavior. As hobbyists, our approaches to keeping these animals can be just as diverse, but they should always be guided by the attempt to understand how they live. Ornamental fish are beautiful, but living, active barbs can easily become a lifelong fascination.

INFORMATION

Judging from the literature available, aquarists like barbs and their relatives a lot more than aquarium writers do. There is a surprising lack of organized, centralized information on this popular group of fishes. The popular aquarium magazines are an excellent source for information on individual species, as is the Internet. Unfortunately, there is no getting around the fact that research into barbs and their relatives can be a slow process, calling for digging in a lot of different sources.

Internet Sites

The commonly available species will be discussed on general aquarium sites, though the quality of that information often makes cross-referencing essential. Danios have a lot of scientific sites dedicated to them, although many look more at DNA than the animals that carry it. Since there are no short cuts, it's no use inventing them. You are best advised to choose a good search engine and work through it, species by species.

There are two sites that are especially useful. The first is a scientific site that offers interesting habitat information on many of our fish. It can be found at:

http://www.fishbase.org

One of the well-established and respected aquarium sites, at:

http://www.fishlinkcentral.com is what the name implies. It's a site that can link you to other more specialized aquarium sites on the Web.

If there is an aquarium club in your area, joining it is a great idea. You can learn a lot about barbs by talking to their keepers.

Books

For books, it is best to support your local pet shop, as they will likely be your most trustworthy source of equipment, advice, and fish. Other good resources for books and book information are:

http://www.barronseduc.com/pets-fish.html
http://www.finleyaquaticbooks.com (mail order aquarium books)
http://www.seahorses.com (mail order aquarium books)

Finding books on barbs and their relatives can be a problem, as you may need to collect an extensive library of general aquarium books to have a wide range of information. Some options are:

Brittan, Dr. Martin R., *Rasboras: Keeping and Breeding Them In Captivity*, Neptune City, NJ. TFH Publications, 1998

Riehl, Dr. Rudiger, Hans A. Baensch, *Aquarium Atlas*, Volume 1, Mergus 1982, U.S. publisher Tetra Press (Division of Warner Lambert) Morris Plains, NJ.

_____. *Aquarium Atlas*, Volume 2, Mergus 1993, U.S. publisher Tetra Press (Division of Warner Lambert) Morris Plains, NJ.

_____. *Aquarium Atlas*, Volume 3, Mergus 1996, U.S. publisher Tetra Press (Division of Warner Lambert) Morris Plains, NJ.

Scheurmann, Ines, *Aquarium Fish Breeding*, Hauppauge, NY, Barron's Educational Series, Inc., 1990.

Schliewen, Ulrich, *Aquarium Fish*, Hauppauge, NY, Barron's Educational Series, Inc., 1992

African barbs, 70–72
Algae eaters, 87–90
Aquarium:
  caves in, 34
  cleaning of, 22, 56
  filtration of, 26–31
  heating of, 15–16
  height of, 14
  lighting of, 15–17
  location of, 15
  maintenance of, 22–23
  plants, 34, 37–39, 42–43
  setting up of, 33–35
  shape of, 14, 18–19
  size of, 13–14
  stand for, 14–15
  stocking of, 17–18
  temperature of, 55
  type of, 18–19
  water of. See Water
Asian barbs, 61–70

Balantiocheilus
  melanopterus, 90–91
Barbels, 7
Barbucca diabolica, 29
Barbus arulius, 63
Barbus callipterus, 71–72
Barbus camptacanthus, 72
Barbus caudovittatus, 9
Barbus conchonius, 19, 63
Barbus cumingii, 63
Barbus denisonii, 40,
  63–65
Barbus dorsalis, 8
Barbus eugrammus, 64
Barbus everetti, 64–65
Barbus fasciatus, 64–65
Barbus fasciolatus, 71
Barbus filamentosus,
  65–66
Barbus gelius, 65–66
Barbus holotaenia, 71
Barbus hulstaerti, 71
Barbus jae, 5, 70–72
Barbus lateristrigata, 66,
  68
Barbus macrops, 9
Barbus narayani, 66, 68

Barbus nigrofasciatus, 60,
  66
Barbus oligolepis, 66–68
Barbus pentazona penta-
  zona, 67
Barbus phutunio, 67
Barbus rhombocellatus,
  53, 67–68
Barbus schwanenfeldii,
  67–68
Barbus semifasciolatus, 8,
  68–69
Barbus stoliczkanus, 69
Barbus tetrazona, 18, 62,
  64
Barbus ticto, 69
Barbus titteya, 8, 69–70
Barbus trimaculatus, 9
Barbus vittatus, 70
Behavior, 13, 19
Bloat, 50
Boraras brigittae, 21, 82
Boraras maculatus, 81–82
Boraras merah, 82
Boraras uropthalmoides,
  82
Botia lecontei, 52
Botia lochachata, 29, 86
Botia macracantha, 86
Botia morleti, 29
Breeding, 58–59
Brine shrimp, 46
Buying, 49–51

Chela caeruleostigmata,
  76
Chela dadyburjori, 20, 76
Chela laubuca, 76–77
Classification, 6–7, 10–11
Compatibility, 19, 35
Crossocheilus siamensis,
  88–89
Crowding, 18

Danio aequipinnatus, 20
Danio albolineatus, 9, 74
Danio choprai, 9, 75
Danio "frankei," 75
Danio kerri, 75

Danio kiyathit, 20, 75
Danio nigrofasciatus, 20,
  75
Danio pathirana, 20,
  75–76
Danio rerio, 18, 73–74
Danio shanensis, 73
Diseases, 54–56

Epalzeorhynchos erythru-
  rus, 91
Epalzeorhynchos
  kallopterus, 89–90
Epiphytic plants, 39, 42

Families, 6
Filters:
  air pump–powered,
    30–31
  canister, 26, 30
  fluidized bed, 31
  outside power, 26, 30
  trickle, 31
  underground, 30
Filtration, 26–27, 31
Fins, 7
Food, 45–46
Fry, 59
Fungus, 55

Garra barreimiae, 56
Garra dembeensis, 52
Garra rufa, 11
Gastromyzon fasciatus, 87
Groups, 18
Gyrinocheilus aymonieri,
  87–88

Habitats, 7
Health, 49–51, 54
Heating, 15–16

Ich, 54–55

Labeo chrysophekadion, 91
Labeo variegatus, 91
Labeo victorianus, 52
Lighting, 15–17
Luciosoma trinema, 92

Medication, 51, 54
Microrasbora erythromi-
  cron, 21, 78
Microrasbora rubescens,
  21, 78
Myxocyprinus asiaticus, 5,
  91–92

Name, 10–11
Neomacheilus botia, 29

Oodinium, 54
Overfeeding, 45

Pangio kuhlii, 29, 86–87
Plants, 37–39, 42–43
Protein skimmers, 31
Pseudogastromyzon
  myersi, 87

Quarantine, 51

Rasbora dorsiocellata, 40,
  83
Rasbora dusonensis, 40
Rasbora kalochroma, 83
Rasboras, 78–85
Rasbora trilineata, 83
Rasbora vaterifloris, 82–83

Sabwa resplendens, 21, 78
Sharks, 90–92
Sundadanio axelrodi, 21,
  82

Tanichthys albonudes, 77
Trigonostigma espei, 81
Trigonostigma hengeli,
  80–81
Trigonostigma heteromor-
  pha, 79–80
Tuberculosis, 56

Velvet, 54

Water, 22, 25–26, 51, 55
White Clouds, 77
White spot, 54–55
Whiteworms, 46

Photo Credits
All photos by Oliver Lucanus.

Cover Photos
All covers by Oliver Lucanus.

Acknowledgments
The authors would like to thank the following individuals, while absolving them of all responsibility for the content: Laurence Azoulay, Pete Liptrot, Andy Taylor, Mary Frauley, Patrick Yap, Dr. Paul V. Loiselle, Frank Greco, Brian Menard, and Takehiro Furuya.

All inquiries should be addressed to:
Barron's Educational Series, Inc.
250 Wireless Boulevard
Hauppauge, NY 11788
http://www.barronseduc.com

Library of Congress Catalog Card No. 2002018598

International Standard Book No. 0-7641-2116-2

Library of Congress Cataloging-in-Publication Data
Elson, Gary.
 The Barbs aquarium : everything about natural history, purchase, health, care, breeding, and species identification / Gary Elson and Oliver Lucanus.
  p. cm.
 Includes bibliographical references (p.).
 ISBN 0-7641-2116-2
  1. Barbs (Fish) I. Lucanus, Oliver. II. Title.

SF458.B3 E48 2002
639.34—dc21   2002018598

Printed in Hong Kong

9 8 7 6 5 4 3 2 1

Important Note
Electrical equipment for aquarium care is described in this book. Please do not fail to read the note below, otherwise serious accidents could occur.

Water damage from broken glass, overflowing, or tank leaks cannot always be avoided. Therefore, you should not fail to take out insurance.

Please take special care that neither children not adults ever eat any aquarium plants. It can result in serious health consequences. Fish medications should always be kept away from children.

Safety Around the Aquarium
Water and electricity can lead to dangerous accidents. Therefore you should make absolutely sure when buying equipment that it is suitable for use in an aquarium.

✔ Every technical device must have the UL sticker on it. These letters give the assurance that the safety of the equipment has been carefully checked by experts and that "with ordinary use" (as the experts say) nothing dangerous can happen.

✔ Always unplug any electrical equipment before you do any cleaning around or in the aquarium.

✔ Never do your own repairs on the aquarium or the equipment if there is something wrong with it. As a matter of safety, all repairs should only be carried out by an expert.